THE GIRL WITH THE AGATE EYES

The Girl with the Agate Eyes

The Untold Story of Mattie Howard, Kansas City's Queen of the Underworld

DAN KELLY

Jacomo Publishing

First Printing, 2023

Cover illustration by Rebecca Wagner.

CONTENTS

Preface

Before the flappers and gun molls of the Jazz Age, there was Mattie Howard. She combined the sexual and fashion freedom that defined the flappers with the gangster-loving lifestyle of the gun molls.

Only Mattie Howard was much more than a gun moll, which typically referred to a girlfriend or wife of a gangster. Mattie was a proper gangster herself.

At the dawn of the Roaring Twenties, she was known as "Queen of the Underworld," "Queen of the Bandits," and the "Golden Girl," and she was described as "the most picturesque woman crook known to police of the Middle West" and "a cold-blooded murderess." But her most common sobriquet was "The Girl with the Agate Eyes."

Mattie associated with many of the Midwest's most notorious criminals, notably the Jones-Lewis gang. Dale Jones, Frank Lewis, and their mates terrorized the Midwest during 1917 and 1918, robbing banks and trains while leaving dead bodies in their wake. The Jones-Lewis gang drew comparisons to the James-Younger gang, which had menaced the same area of the country a half-century earlier.

Mattie had a link to that gang as well. Jesse E. James, who was usually referred to as Jesse James Jr., practiced law in Kansas City for about fifteen years. The son of perhaps the nation's most notorious outlaw represented many of the area's gangsters, including Mattie Howard.

This book focuses on the period from May 1918 to November 1921, when Mattie's saga captivated Kansas City, Missouri, and made headlines around the nation. Her story included manhunts, shootouts,

1

killings, love affairs, and murder trials as it sprawled across multiple states. Newspapers played up the succession of Mattie's supposed doomed lovers, and men did, in fact, have a habit of suffering violent deaths after associating with her.

The amount of coverage and the depth of details dwarf anything a twenty-first century newspaper would publish.

As much attention as she received, Mattie didn't become a national legend like many gangsters — almost all male — who came along when Prohibition-era bootlegging and its associated crimes escalated into a national scourge in the 1920s and early 1930s. Americans had more important things on their minds and in their newspapers in 1918, when Mattie's name first splashed across front pages.

Things like the Great War, later to be known as World War I, which left an estimated sixteen million soldiers and civilians dead. And the 1918 influenza pandemic, which killed another fifty million world-wide, including about 675,000 in the United States.

Despite such suffering and tragedy in the world, Mattie and her fellow gangsters went about their business of robbing and, in some cases, killing. In Kansas City, they got away with it at an alarming rate. With dishonest politicians and corrupt cops, the city was an oasis for outlaws.

Kansas City also was, like most American big cities, entering a period of social and sexual freedom for women as men marched off to war and women replaced them in the workplace. Society had changed tremendously since the prudish Victorian Era of the late nineteenth century, growing more permissive — or at least less intolerant — with the explosion of movie theaters, dance halls, jazz clubs, and vaudeville houses. These were the germination days for the Jazz Age and the emergence of flappers, who smoked, drank, flirted, and flaunted their sexuality.

Given such a wide-open atmosphere, it made sense that an independent woman such as Mattie Howard wound up becoming Kansas City's Girl with the Agate Eyes.

Her story has long since faded into near oblivion, however. The only substantive work on her is the 1937 book *The Pathway of Mattie Howard (To and from Prison): True Story of the Regeneration of an Ex-Convict and Gangster Woman.* The name "M. Harris" appears on the cover, but in most quarters the book is considered an autobiography written in the third person. "M. Harris" almost certainly refers to Mary Belle Harris, a leading promoter of prison reform who at the time was superintendent of the nation's first federal correctional institution for women. She wrote *I Knew Them in Prison* (1936), but her role in the Mattie Howard book isn't clear.

The Pathway of Mattie Howard provides insights into our protagonist's life, especially about her days in the Missouri State Penitentiary, but it leaves out major facts that might reflect badly on her — such as marrying a man when she was seventeen, then leaving him to join a gangster boyfriend in Kansas City. The book also includes details that research shows to be inaccurate (it claims she associated with Al Capone, John Dillinger, and "Pretty Boy" Floyd) and other details that are difficult to believe (she was arrested eighteen times in one day ... really?).

Publications of the period, in particular the Kansas City newspapers — *The Star, The Post,* and *The Journal* — are more reliable sources for the Mattie Howard story.

The tale on these pages is told through an anonymous first-person narrator but is presented from the perspective of William Moorhead. A native Kansas Citian who was a high school buddy of baseball legend Casey Stengel, Moorhead served as a police reporter for *The Kansas City Star* for more than fifty years, starting in 1913.

Moorhead, who briefly took a cub reporter named Ernest Hemingway under his wing, likely wrote the bulk of *The Star's* stories about Mattie Howard, as well as about other Kansas City gangsters of the era. (It probably was not a coincidence that Dale Jones' final alias was "David Moorhead.") *The Star* didn't put bylines atop articles in those days, however, so there's no way to know what Moorhead wrote and what he didn't.

The lone exception was a June 6, 1919, article that contained the first reference to Mattie Howard's "agate eyes." It was, according to Moorhead himself, authored by Marcel Wallenstein, who went on to cover the Normandy invasion, Hitler's death, and many other major stories for The Star. Moorhead wrote in a 1951 bylined story that Wallenstein had produced the 1919 "agate eyes" article, also indicating that he (Moorhead) had written "many news accounts about ... 'The Girl with the Agate Eyes.'"

This first-person narrative supposes that Moorhead wrote all The Star's significant uncredited stories about Mattie Howard. Aside from that bit of literary license, everything on these pages is nonfiction. All the facts, quotes, and anecdotes were drawn from accounts in newspapers, books, other publications, or public records. No events were fabricated.

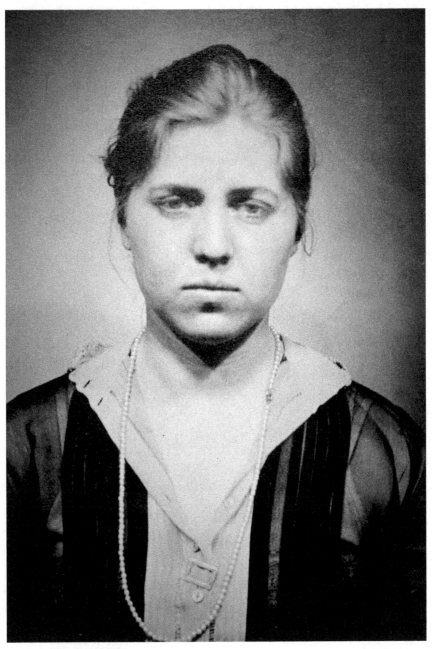

Mattie Howard
Smith Archive / Alamy Stock Photo

Prologue: Kansas City, 1953

If I'm being honest, I was infatuated with Mattie Howard, just like every other poor dumb sap who crossed paths with her.

But at least I didn't wind up dead like most of the other poor dumb saps.

Our relationship was strictly professional. I was a reporter, and she was the subject of my stories. But that didn't keep me from falling for her. She was smart, playful, frank, well-spoken, witty, and flirty.

In short, she was a great interview. And easy on the eyes, too.

Thirty-five years after meeting Mattie Howard — always her full name; I could never bring myself to use just her last name like we newspaper reporters are supposed to — I still daydream about the first time I saw her.

It was June 22, 1918. Blond hair framed her face as she leaned through an open window of a train stopped at the Topeka station. She was returning to Kansas City to face a murder charge, and I was there to board the train, trying to get her story before any other reporters could.

I was only twenty-six, three years older than Mattie. Still, I was hardly wet behind the ears. I had worked for *The Kansas City Star* for nearly ten years, starting as an office boy and taking over as a police reporter when I was twenty-one. Forty years later, I'm still at it.

If there's one thing I've learned in that time, it's that you can't trust the cops any more than the crooks.

The police said Mattie was a criminal mastermind who not only associated with some of the Midwest's most notorious outlaws but also was the brains behind their operations in our wide-open gangster haven of Kansas City, Missouri. "She often was referred to by detectives and attorneys as the 'most dangerous criminal ever in Kansas City,'" *The Kansas City Post* wrote.

That was hyperbole, but when it came to Mattie Howard, all of us played fast and loose with the truth at times. She was, after all, a hell of a story.

Those years were the golden age for cop reporters. We not only worked out of an office right in the police station, but we also enjoyed virtually unfettered access to crime scenes, suspects, and witnesses. In fact, I testified at more than one trial because I had reached a crime scene before the police or had uncovered evidence they hadn't.

I also witnessed the cops doing things that wouldn't fly today. The accepted methods of extracting a confession included battering prisoners with chairs, slashing them with belts, and pounding them with rubber hoses. Some interrogators favored a bar of laundry soap in a sock as their weapon of choice. I occasionally peeked through a cracked-open door to watch the questioning, but the cops didn't mind if we reporters walked right in during the torture. They knew we'd keep quiet.

Police naturally reserved those kinds of beatings for men. We reporters, on the other hand, gave no special treatment to the fairer sex.

Women who robbed and murdered made for such good copy that we jumped at every opportunity to write about them — and to anoint them with catchy nicknames. That helps explain the immense amount of coverage *The Star* and other Kansas City newspapers gave to Mattie.

My clippings are yellowed and tattered now, as are the articles from the competition, *The Post* and *The Journal*. I figure I should put my memories of Mattie on paper now, before they fade like the print on those old clippings.

| 1 |

Raton, New Mexico

"Crashing and rending of wood awakened us, and here were detectives bent on finding me. You would think from their actions they were looking for some wild beast of the jungle, ferocious and dangerous."
Mattie Howard, *Linn County Budget-Gazette*, June 28, 1933

Mattie Howard knew Sam Taylor was a gambler, a bootlegger, a thief, and an ex-con. She knew he had served time in the federal penitentiary in Leavenworth. Twice.

Sam Taylor
National Archives

But Sam Taylor — or was he going by George Davis, Jim Davis, Jim Jimmerson, Jim Robinson, Frank Cook, Frank Thomas, William J. Hall, or just plain Whitey these days? — was sweet on Mattie, and that's what really mattered.

He even said he was willing to help her try to free her true love, Albert Pagel, who was in jail (under the name George Moore) in Springfield, Missouri.

Of course, Mattie didn't tell her mother any of this.

To Martha Howard, Mattie was a good girl, albeit with a bit of a wild streak, even if she had visited her mother only once in recent years, and that visit hadn't gone well.

Mattie was here now, in Martha's home on Pigeon Street in Raton, a tiny town tucked in the mountains of northeast New Mexico just a few miles south of the Colorado border. Mattie had spent virtually her entire childhood in Colorado — Denver to be precise — although she ran away from home more than once as a teenager.

That was before she got married just days short of her eighteenth birthday to a man named Frank J. Vanders. Now it was five-and-a-half years later, and, though Mattie was still married, divorce proceedings had begun.

So at this point, Mattie had a husband, a lover, and a male companion, the last of whom had joined her in her mother's house in Raton.

They had arrived from Picher, Oklahoma, where Sam Taylor was well known for his extra-legal activities. Mattie and Sam probably figured nobody would know them in tiny Raton.

Martha Howard didn't much care for the looks of Sam Taylor, whom she described as "an unattractive man, heavyset and coarse-looking." That didn't prevent Mrs. Howard from offering the ruffian food and lodging for at least one night.

Sam and Mattie had driven a few miles north in search of entertainment in the larger town of Trinidad, Colorado, and after returning, Mrs. Howard allowed Sam to use the bed in her son's room.

Within hours, Mattie Howard's life would be turned upside down.

The next morning, Monday, June 18, 1918, Mattie was in her mother's bedroom.

Six policemen stationed themselves around the outside of the house at about 6:30 a.m., prepared for a possible escape attempt, as two detectives banged on the door of the little house in Raton.

When Mrs. Howard opened up and saw the badges, she assumed the law was after Sam Taylor.

But no.

"Is Mattie Howard here?" one of the detectives asked.

"Why, yes," Mrs. Howard answered.

"Where is she?"

Mrs. Howard pointed toward her bedroom.

The detectives barged through the door and found Mattie, still wearing her night clothes.

"The chief wants to talk to you, Mattie. Will you come and see him without any trouble?"

"Sure," Mattie replied.

She wasn't particularly afraid. She almost never was. Solidly built and tall enough to look most men right in their eyes, Mattie had always been able to take care of herself.

She didn't say anything when the detectives told her to get dressed, then watched her do so.

After collecting Mattie, the detectives checked her brother's room and found Sam Taylor fully dressed — and with a loaded revolver.

By now, neighbors had assembled outside, and they watched as the officers led Mattie and Sam Taylor out the front door to the waiting squad cars.

Still not sure what was happening, Mrs. Howard, could only watch, too.

"Don't worry, honey," she said to Mattie. "Everything will be all right. God is still on the throne."

Why sure, Mattie told the Trinidad police, she knew Joe Morino. But that didn't mean she killed him.

And, yes, she had been in Kansas City in late May, but that didn't make her a murderer.

But somebody had killed the wealthy jewelry dealer known as Diamond Joe — had bludgeoned him to death after tying him to a bed with baling wire and had left his bloody corpse in a Kansas City hotel room, taking diamonds worth about $2,000 and a large amount of cash — and much of the evidence found by the Kansas City police suggested Mattie Howard was involved.

Now the Trinidad police had found letters in Mattie's grip that referred to diamonds in her possession and negotiations for their sale.

Mattie professed her innocence, claiming she had an alibi that would clear her, although anything she said to the Trinidad police mattered very little anyway. The wheels of the legal system already were in motion, and Mattie Howard was about to be run over.

If Mattie was surprised the law had come looking for her, she shouldn't have been. She had been the subject of a national search for several weeks. With most of the nation's attention on the Great War in Europe, where U.S. soldiers had been fighting for more than a year now, Mattie might have been the most wanted woman in America.

Small stories about the diamond king's murder in Kansas City had been interspersed among the many updates on the war in newspapers across the country.

Meanwhile, the Kansas City police had issued a circular seeking Mattie Howard and offering a reward for her arrest. Her name — if not her face — was well known among law enforcement around the nation.

The circular described Mattie as attractive, fashionably dressed, blue eyes, blond hair, five feet ten inches, and 155 pounds.

Given her physical attributes, especially her height and her blond hair, Mattie stood out in a crowd. Add her piercing blue eyes and assertive personality, and she was the type of woman people — men in particular — tended to remember.

That was too bad for Mattie.

It turned out a Trinidad restaurant keeper, who had cashed a check for her on April 4 during her previous visit to her mother's home, saw her again in Trinidad on June 16. He had heard of the Morino murder, knew of Mattie's alleged role in it, and told the police of her presence in Trinidad.

They grabbed her the next morning at her mother's house.

Mattie had used her own name when she was in Trinidad in early April, but on this visit she was going by Anna Brooks. That was the name she gave the Trinidad police, even though they knew her real name.

All of which suggests Mattie was a woman on the run. On the other hand, if she knew she was a wanted woman and was trying to hide from the law, her mother's house would seem to be one of the first places the police would look.

In any case, she was now in the Trinidad jail, and the Trinidad police had wired their Kansas City counterparts to tell them they had their woman. Two Kansas City police detectives were on their way to pick her up.

The Trinidad police obtained a fugitive warrant to hold Mattie (as well as Sam Taylor), so she sat in a cell in Trinidad, waiting.

Her mother was allowed to see her, and during one of Mrs. Howard's visits, a police sergeant showed Mattie a telegram from J.L. Ghent, Kansas City's acting police chief. It read: "HOLD MATTIE HOWARD WANTED FOR FIRST DEGREE MURDER KANSAS CITY OFFICERS ENROUTE."

Showing no emotion, she returned the telegram to the officer, who said, "Well, you don't seem much concerned."

"It doesn't concern me," Mattie replied.

Her mother asked, "Did you do this, honey?"

"No, no," Mattie said. "I don't know a thing about it."

"Honey, I believe you," Mrs. Howard said.

* * *

When Kansas City detectives Harry Arthur and Denver Mitchell arrived by train on June 20, they weren't alone. They brought with them Ira Allen, a porter at the Touraine Apartment Hotel, where Joe Morino was murdered.

Allen had told police he had shown Morino and a blond woman to their room two days before Morino's bloody body was found there. Arthur and Mitchell figured he could identify Mattie Howard as the blond in question.

The Kansas City detectives marched Mattie in front of Allen in the Trinidad jail.

"That's the woman," the porter exclaimed. He also said he recognized her voice.

Mattie said nothing in response.

The next day, Arthur and Mitchell put handcuffs and shackles on Mattie and Sam Taylor, hauled them to the Trinidad rail depot and escorted them — and Ira Allen — onto the train to Kansas City.

The 555-mile trip east went through the night and into the day of June 22. That gave the detectives plenty of time to try to pry information from their two prisoners.

I joined the traveling company of two detectives, two suspects and a witness when the train pulled into Topeka, Kansas.

Here's a portion of my June 23, 1918, story:

The Pullman stopped for five minutes at Topeka. A pretty, slender girl passed under the car windows. She wore a Red Cross insignia on her white hat. She offered flowers for sale that more money might be obtained for the comfort of American soldiers abroad. A hand reached from a car window and the fingers pulled a bouquet from the flower basket. Mattie Howard tossed a coin to the smiling flower girl.

I traveled with the group the final sixty miles to Kansas City's Union Station, and the detectives grilled their prisoners virtually the entire way while Ira Allen sat silently with them.

"Suitcases were piled about (Allen's) feet," I wrote, "and from his lips protruded a long unlighted cigar with a wide band and bearing the inscription, 'Saddle Rock Saloon Special.'"

Detective Arthur questioned Mattie while Detective Mitchell worked on Taylor.

Mitchell was positioned next to Taylor, who kept a newspaper over his manacled hands. Taylor said that at the time of the murder he had been in Picher, Oklahoma, which he insisted was where he first met Mattie just three weeks earlier.

"Saw her walking down the street and fell in love at first sight," Taylor said. "I took her around places, then asked her to marry me. She said no, that she had a husband living up at Trinidad. I persuaded her to go there and see about her divorce. We went and we got pinched."

Taylor claimed he had been in Kansas City only once, about a year earlier, and said he had never heard of Morino.

"You have got me wrong. I'm a gambler, not a killer. Why, do you know I've kept from killing a half dozen men in my 33 years of life — just because of my gentle nature?"

Detective Mitchell wondered why, then, he was carrying a revolver when the Trinidad police nabbed him.

"I had the gat to protect myself in case Mattie's husband showed up and wanted battle. But I wouldn't hurt anyone if I could get out of it some other way. Honest. Say, I'm a gambler, and a good one at that. Made five thousand bucks shooting craps in Oklahoma last year. Yes, and I spent it all on women."

I also eavesdropped as Mattie talked with Detective Arthur. She stuck to the story she had told the Trinidad officers.

"I tell you I'm innocent! I knew Joe Morino — had business dealings with him. Never saw him outside his pawnshop. I never went to places of amusement with him and most assuredly was not his 'sweetheart.' I did not murder Morino, don't know who did, and never was in the Touraine Hotel in my life."

Mattie freely provided details to Arthur about her childhood, saying she was born on a farm in Idaho and moved with her family to Denver when she was a baby.

Saying she was a "tom boy," she related a story that she claimed was her only previous brush with the law. She was at a street fight between rival gangs, she said, urging on the combatants when a patrolman arrived on the scene. He broke up the fight and arrested Mattie, though she was released with a reprimand.

She also recounted her marriage to Frank Vanders, her subsequent unhappy married life, their separation, and her arrival in Kansas City in 1917.

"I was all alone, and I craved a good time," she told Arthur. "Several girls urged me to go to cabarets. They introduced me to nice boys, and we went to the cafés a great deal. No wonder I couldn't hold a job!"

Arthur's investigations in the preceding days had revealed that Mattie had made a deposit of $600 in a bank in late February, and that only fifteen dollars remained.

How, he wondered, could a working girl have accumulated $600 so quickly?

"I borrowed the money," she said, "from a good friend."

That friend no doubt was Albert Pagel, known to the detectives as George Moore.

At one point, as the train chugged through the eastern Kansas farm-land, Taylor addressed the object of his affections, and Arthur took advantage of it to stir things up between Mattie and Sam.

"Mattie, when we get out of this trouble, (how about) you and me gets married, and we'll live in a little house down on one of these here farms and raise kids and everything," Taylor said. "What do you say?"

Her answer was a sneer.

Arthur jumped in.

"Did you tell your friend Sam about your other sweetheart in jail at Springfield, Missouri, for motor car stealing?" he asked Mattie.

"How'd you find out about him?" she replied.

"I trailed you by wire after you left Kansas City late in May to Springfield, then found that you were friendly with a man named Moore, who was in jail under heavy bond. You couldn't get Moore out of jail, so you went to Joplin and Tulsa, and met a rich oil man who was about ready to lend you some bond money, when you left town suddenly. Moore's still in jail. He was there, too, at the time Morino was killed, else ..."

"Don't try to drag that man into this mess!" Mattie exclaimed. "I love that man — the only one I ever loved. He's the only man I'd ever marry again."

Taylor overheard that part, and his face soured. The detectives laughed.

Arthur returned to details of the murder, asking Mattie when and where she met Joe Morino.

"It was in April," she said. "I observed him often in a restaurant next door to his pawnshop. I took my meals there when I stopped at the Sherman (Hotel). Morino would smile and bow to me. Once I asked the restaurant to cash a ten-dollar check. He refused but sent me to the pawnshop of Morino. I bought a small ring for four dollars and thus got the check cashed.

"I returned several times to the pawnshop and bought things — just small things — a wristwatch and such. Yes, I gave checks in payment. And they were all good ones, too."

The Kansas City police had evidence that proved otherwise.

They said Morino had been given a check for a hundred dollars, signed "Mrs. M. Howard," in payment for a diamond brooch two weeks before his death. The bank returned the check to Morino, indicating "No account here."

"No, I never bought a diamond brooch," Mattie said. "And never wrote a bad check for a hundred dollars. And Joe always treated me as a gentleman should treat a lady."

Detective Arthur didn't push her on the matter, instead asking if she feared the outcome of her trial.

"I should say not!" she answered. "I'm innocent and ..."

"Where were you the latter part of May, when Morino was killed?" the detective interrupted, as the train pulled into Union Station.

"That's for me to know and you to find out. I know where I was but won't tell. But understand me, I had nothing to do with Morino's death. And I'm not worried about the trial.

"The notoriety will do me good. Look at Evelyn Nesbit Thaw."

Obviously, Mattie was planning for life in the public eye.

Evelyn Nesbit Thaw was a chorus girl who a decade earlier had become entangled in a notorious murder case that led to what was called the "Trial of the Century." The accused was her wealthy husband, Harry Thaw, who had killed famed architect Stanford White in front of dozens of witnesses.

Thaw's motive revolved around Evelyn's earlier relationship with the much older White.

White had wooed Evelyn when she was just 14, keeping her in a room covered in red velvet, with a swing hanging from the ceiling. The murder and trial made front-page news from coast to coast, so she became a national celebrity. Newspapers referred to her as "The Girl in the Red Velvet Swing."

Evelyn went on to star in several movies from 1914 through 1922, including the semi-autobiographical "Redemption" in 1917. By the time of Mattie's arrest in June 1918, Evelyn Nesbit Thaw had been a celebrity for more than a decade.

But as Mattie considered dipping her toe into that world of celebrity, she might have overlooked one important detail in comparing herself to Evelyn Nesbit Thaw: Whereas Evelyn was married to a murder suspect, Mattie *was* one.

| 2 |

Denver

"When I was a little girl six years of age, my home was so crowded that mother put us girls in a Catholic convent and paid for us. I have heard people say very unkind things about the nuns, but I think they are a very humble, sacrificing little group."
Mattie Howard, *Foursquare Crusader*, May 26, 1937

Mattie Howard's father was a drunk, her mother a religious zealot. Mattie would grow up to be both, though not simultaneously.

First, she was simply a curious little girl.

Born Martha Alice Howard on November 11, 1894, in Preston, Idaho, she was the oldest girl, with two older brothers, among Charles and Martha E. Howard's twelve children — six of whom died during infancy or childhood.

The family, which moved to Denver before Mattie was a year old, struggled to survive on Charles Howard's salary as a railroad man. As an adult, Mattie would say her "father drank up most of his wages and brought little home other than his sodden self."

Martha Howard, who married Charles on July 4, 1887, in Beaverhead, Washington, when she was eighteen and he was forty-one, had spent four years during her youth in a convent. She decided Mattie and her younger sister Marie would follow the same path, even though they weren't being raised as Catholics.

Marie returned home after only a few days, but Mattie took a liking to life with the nuns at St. Mary's Academy in Denver.

The school for girls was founded in 1864 by three Sisters of Loretto who had traveled north from Santa Fe, New Mexico. St. Mary's, which continues to operate, boasts wealthy socialite Margaret "Molly" Brown as an early benefactor.

Mattie continued at St. Mary's, returning home during the summers, until she was in high school.

"I loved the peace and serenity I found at the convent, away from the noisy brood of brothers and smaller sisters at home," she said. "The nuns were kind to me, and I made my first communion in the church.

"I learned to sing there. And to sew and tat and have a sense of order of things."

Mattie converted to Catholicism and even became a nun — at least in her make-believe world. She would place a cloth over her head, press her hands together in prayer, fix her eyes toward heaven, and preach to her brothers and sisters.

By the age of eleven, Mattie was showing that she was both creative and independent.

Her mother gave her ten cents each Sunday, and Mattie developed a weekly routine. She purchased a roundtrip ticket on the electric streetcar for a nickel and rode alone to Denver's newly updated Union Station. With her remaining five cents, she bought salted peanuts.

Then she planted herself on a bench in Union Station's great hall, eating peanuts while concocting stories about the rail travelers she watched coming and going. This woman was returning home from a trip to Europe. That man was meeting his bride-to-be.

As a gaggle of five or six children trailed a matronly lady, who wiped their faces and fed them lunches, Mattie imagined that the mother was about to introduce her offspring to the man who would become their father. Mattie, yet to be introduced to the birds and the bees, thought the children had arrived in the world with no biological contribution from a man.

After several of her Sunday visits to Union Station, the depot master began to notice the blond girl who passed her afternoons in the company of no friends or family members and with no apparent purpose. He approached Mattie, indicated he was concerned about her safety, and asked her name. She refused to give it or any other personal information.

"It's none of your business," she said.

Ultimately, he had someone follow Mattie home, putting an end to her excursions when Mrs. Howard found out about them.

Two years later, Mattie actually delivered a baby. No, not her own.

A doctor was delayed in reaching the Howards' home when it was time for her brother Leon to arrive in this world. Still ignorant of the facts of life and previously unaware that her mother even was pregnant, Mattie took charge.

"I thought my mother was dying," she said.

After locating a medical book in the house, Mattie found the child-birth chapter, which included a picture of a baby and a white rose.

"Leon didn't look like any rose. He looked like a drowned rat," she said. "It said to cover him with sweet oil, so I figured salt pork drippings were the best we had in that line, and I greased him up with that. When the doctor did get there, the baby was burnt raw with the salt in the fat."

Leon survived the ordeal, and the doctor complimented thirteen-year-old Mattie on her efforts.

As she matured into her teens, Mattie "developed into a beautiful girl." That's according to the 1937 book *The Pathway of Mattie Howard*, which is written in the third person and credits "M. Harris" on the cover. It's no secret that Mattie wrote the book, however, and she wasn't shy about including details that are questionable at best.

The Pathway of Mattie Howard said that by the time Mattie was sixteen, she had "a well-formed figure, large expressive eyes enhanced by dark eyebrows and long, dark eyelashes which formed a pleasing contrast to her blondness" as well as "fair skin, nicely modeled nose, and a full, sensitive mouth denoting affection." Mattie's photo appeared in advertising for tooth powder, the book said, and she won a beauty contest in which 500 teen blonds competed, earning a trip to Europe that her mother forbade her to take.

More from the book:

She worked at a candy factory, where a young man "annoyed her with ungentlemanly remarks" and she dumped a barrel of jelly beans on him. She threw a cup at her father when he insulted her mother and, while training to be a nurse at a Denver hospital, launched a bedpan at a doctor who reprimanded her.

Meanwhile, teenage Mattie developed a passion for fun that put her at odds with her mother.

"Evenings I wanted to dance and go to the movies and have a good time, and, when mother remonstrated, I fussed and fumed to be allowed to do as I pleased," she said later in life. "When telling the truth got me in trouble, I soon learned to fib about where I had been."

After one of Mattie's nights out, Martha Howard caught her returning home in the wee hours and confronted her.

"Mattie, you aren't a bad girl," Mrs. Howard said, "but you will be if you keep on."

The message didn't sink in.

Mattie later said: "When Mother would correct me and advise me against going to certain places of amusement, I'd say, 'Don't tell me that; those ideas belong back in 1860; they're out of date.'"

One movie she saw inspired her. It starred Mary Pickford as a young woman who was unhappy at home so she left for the big city and found good fortune.

Mattie ran away, but not to a big city. She went to Limon, Colorado — about ninety miles southeast of Denver with a population of perhaps 1,000 — and took a job as a candy-and-cigar girl and waitress at a railroad station. That escapade lasted only a few weeks before she returned home.

Mattie then worked at "several other positions in small towns in Colorado" before leaving home for good and moving to Kansas City, according to *The Pathway of Mattie Howard*. That's far from the whole truth, however.

By age seventeen, Mattie was back home full time.

She might have remained at the convent forever except her mother became ill. Mattie reluctantly left the nuns behind and took over most of the duties around the house while attending services at a Catholic Church, singing in the church choir, and continuing to enjoy her social life.

At some point she met Frank J. Vanders.

The Pathway of Mattie Howard doesn't mention Vanders by name, but it says she "became acquainted with a very nice young man" who soon proposed marriage. She said yes but, according to the book, quickly realized her mistake, ran away, and went into hiding for nine months. After returning home, Mattie supposedly told her suitor she wanted nothing to do with him, and he unsuccessfully attempted suicide.

Call it a fable. Or maybe a parable.

The truth is that seventeen-year-old Mattie Howard and twenty-two-year-old Frank J. Vanders, a Navy veteran, were married on November 2, 1912, in Denver, where they maintained an address for the next three years.

We know few other details about the marriage other than that Mattie and Frank spent most of 1916 and 1917 in the Detroit area, a fact confirmed by records from the federal penitentiary in Leavenworth, Kansas. That's where Mattie's brother Oliver served a three-and-a-half-year sentence after pleading guilty to robbing a post office in Walsenburg, Colorado.

Mattie's name appears repeatedly in Oliver Howard's records, which notes every piece of mail he sent or received while in Leavenworth. The notations include dates and addresses of those with whom he corresponded. Mattie's letters came mostly from Colorado in late 1915, then from Detroit or nearby towns through March 1917.

Those records pinpoint Mattie's whereabouts just before her arrival in Kansas City. Moreover, Oliver Howard's incarceration served as perhaps the most important factor in Mattie's descent into the criminal underworld.

If not for Oliver's crime and punishment, she never would have met Albert Pagel.

* * *

Oliver Howard and Albert Pagel were Army buddies — and much more.

Both were privates in Troop F of the Fifth U.S. Cavalry, which was stationed at Fort Leavenworth but was assigned to southern Colorado in late 1914 during the so-called Colorado Coalfield War.

About 10,000 coal miners had gone on strike in September 1913, citing years of poor working conditions. Dozens of people died in the ensuing violence. President Woodrow Wilson sent in federal troops in April 1914, shortly after two women, eleven children and twelve men were killed during the infamous Ludlow Massacre.

The federal troops helped quell the violence, but the strike didn't end until December 1914. Troops remained through the end of the year.

Oliver Howard saw the situation as an opportunity.

He was far from a model soldier after enlisting in March 1912. He had faced a summary court several times for drunkenness, and in December 1914 he had recently rejoined his troop after being held four months awaiting court martial for the theft of a revolver. He was acquitted on the theft charge but convicted of having stolen property in his possession.

Somehow, his superior officers trusted Howard to be the mail orderly for Troop F, assigned to take the camp's mail to the post office in Walsenburg, Colorado, and to pick up incoming packages there.

While at the post office December 1, Howard noticed assistant postmaster Agapito Peter Atencio toss two registered packages containing cash into an unlocked and partly open drawer even though the office had a safe.

"If a man had that much money, he sure wouldn't have to work anymore," Howard said to Atencio.

The packages contained $15,000.

The next day, the postmaster discovered the money missing and went to Troop F's camp to tell officers of the theft and of Oliver Howard's remark. A search produced $4,850 in Howard's bunk and another $1,430 under a pile of straw in the stables, but the remaining $8,720 in stolen cash was never found.

At first, Howard played dumb, denying he was involved and refusing to make a statement. He was turned over to civil authorities and taken to the Huerfano County Jail in Walsenburg. Meanwhile, officials discovered that Pagel and fellow private Samuel F. Mortimore had been missing from camp the night of the robbery.

Within two weeks of the robbery, which created quite a sensation both in Walsenburg and at Fort Leavenworth, Howard confessed and implicated Pagel and Mortimer. All three wound up pleading guilty in federal court in Denver on March 19, 1915. Three other soldiers who had been arrested and accused of helping hide the loot were tried, but they were acquitted.

As the mastermind, Howard received a three-and-half-year sentence; Pagel and Mortimore got two-and-a-half years.

Mattie would insist later that she didn't know Albert Pagel before she settled in Kansas City. If so, that would be one huge coincidence.

Pagel arrived at the Leavenworth penitentiary March 21, 1915, the same day as Oliver Howard. At one point, I wrote that Mattie met Albert in 1917 while she was visiting Oliver at the penitentiary and that they became so enamored with each other they made plans to run off together. Since learning more about Mattie's background, I've concluded it's more likely they had met while Pagel and Oliver Howard served together in the Army.

Mattie was home alone in Denver while her husband was in Navy hospitals for much of 1914 and 1915. For part of that time, Pagel and Oliver Howard were stationed within 160 miles of Denver in Walsenburg during the Colorado coal miners' strike and riots. Also, Mattie had one sister who lived in Walsenburg and another in nearby La Veta, Colorado.

The federal prison records of Albert Pagel Jr. from March 1915 tell us the following:

He was twenty-four years old, stood five feet, nine-and-half inches tall, and weighed 166 pounds.

He was born in New York City and still listed it as his residence.

He was a Methodist. His father was born in Germany and his mother in Norway. Both were dead.

He had a sister, Carey N. Pagel, who lived in Brooklyn.

He was reprimanded regularly for disobeying prison rules.

Leavenworth's records included a description of Pagel's work ethic on June 3, 1916: "This prisoner is reported for extreme laziness and continually shirking work. He quits work and seats himself whenever he feels like doing so. ... The work performed by this man amounts to practically nothing."

Then, on July 26, 1916, the records described how he refused to accept overalls issued to him, insisting on a new pair. "I hate like hell to wear other men's old clothes," he told a prison guard.

Nevertheless, Pagel wound up serving less than two years of his two-and-a-half-year sentence, receiving his discharge on March 2, 1917.

About that date ...

Mattie's letters to her brother, which had arrived fairly regularly during Oliver's first two years of imprisonment, ceased in March 1917 even though Oliver remained in Leavenworth until November 27, 1917.

At some point, Mattie left Frank J. Vanders behind in Detroit and headed to Kansas City. The exact date of Mattie's arrival is unclear, but she was listed in the 1917 city directory as living at 4936 Agnes Avenue.

Also landing in Kansas City at about that time: Albert Pagel.

He and Mattie reached Kansas City shortly before the onset of the Spanish Flu of 1918 and likely within weeks of when the United States entered World War I on April 6, 1917. Neither had any apparent ties to the city, but it probably seemed like the logical destination for a man with Pagel's skillset and demeanor.

* * *

In 1917, prisoners didn't emerge from the Leavenworth federal penitentiary and head to Kansas City merely to take in the sights.

The trip is thirty-four miles by car (twenty-four miles as the crow flies) along the Missouri River, then across the Big Muddy where it takes a sharp turn to the east en route to St. Louis. Many newly freed ex-cons hopped on the interurban electric railway that operated between Leavenworth and Kansas City. It made for a quick journey from the convict's purgatory at Leavenworth to the criminal's Garden of Eden in Kansas City.

Although designated officially as the "Heart of America" by the City Council in 1915, Kansas City soon thereafter also earned the nickname "Paris of the Plains." The moniker stuck not because the Missouri city shared the French capital's reputation for food, fashion, and romance, but rather its notoriety for gambling, prostitution, and corruption.

Kansas City came by its reputation dishonestly.

It had been a lawless town dating to the days of Jesse James. By the twentieth century, it was at the center of a swath of the country running from Texas to North Dakota that evolved from the Wild West into a criminal playground that fostered outlaws who sometimes roamed the entire region, especially after automobiles came into common use.

As many Eastern cities cracked down on crime early in the new century, Kansas City cranked up instead.

* * *

Lear B. Reed was a cop who took on the challenge of cleaning up the decades-old corruption in 1939, when he became chief of police in Kansas City after having served as an FBI special agent there. He described his experiences in *Human Wolves: Seventeen Years of War on Crime* (1941).

Reed wrote that the city possessed "a foul mire of corruption, both within and without the police department — and worse, each linked with the other," and that "the Bowery, the Barbary Coast, Chinatown, the Orient, Singapore, and other notorious spots on the globe that have been in the spotlight of fact or fancy — none of them had anything on Kansas City."

A prime example of the police force's corruption occurred just before Mattie and Albert Pagel arrived in Kansas City. In February 1917, city police commissioners fired eighty-seven employees, including four sergeants, four detectives, and forty-seven patrolmen, because they got on the wrong side of Police Chief Hiram W. Hammil.

Three officers were dismissed after taking a stand against Hammil when he released a man who had been arrested "for attacking little girls," according to *The Star*. Two members of the vice squad made the mistake of raiding "the most notorious resorts in the city." "Resort" was a euphemism for a house of prostitution.

And John R. McCall, a sergeant at the Woodland Avenue Station, was second on the list of the dismissed officers despite (or because of) having "the reputation of being a strong crusader against vice and the underworld."

"McCall crossed Chief Hammil recently by raiding the home of 'Jack' Boyle, ex-convict and a close friend of the chief's," *The Star* reported. "The raiders found an opium layout. Boyle at the time boasted that he had a 'pull' with Chief Hammil, and that McCall would lose his job."

So perhaps it was not surprising that criminals not only felt free to ply their trade in Kansas City, but they also fled there after robbing banks or trains or committing other crimes in the surrounding region, knowing they could find refuge.

"Kansas City in those days was the 'lam town' for the crooks of half a continent," said one of several syndicated Sunday supplement stories that spread the legend of Mattie Howard in newspapers nationwide. "If warrants became too numerous and 'dicks' too inquisitive in Chicago, St. Louis, Denver, El Paso, and even San Francisco, the 'wanted' in the underworld retreated to 'K.C.' The Mid-Western metropolis became the rendezvous for the bad men of a dozen states."

For example, in May 1919, three men who had been arrested for stealing a car in nearby Lafayette County, Missouri, killed a city marshal and his two deputies to escape custody. They rushed to Kansas City and disappeared into the underworld, never to be found.

When Albert Pagel and Mattie arrived in Kansas City, Pagel entered the perfect environment to rekindle his criminal ways and Mattie embarked on an entirely new direction in her life. She later called Pagel her one true love, saying, "I did everything for him and would go to any depth that I might have his love."

Turned out that depth was pretty deep.

| 3 |

Dale Jones

"Last year one of the worst bandit gangs that has existed since the time of the James boys was broken up … most of the members being killed or captured. This gang was known as the Jones gang, the leader being Dale Jones, who is reputed to have successfully held up twenty-three banks and no one knows how many other institutions."
Arms and the Man, The Official Organ of the National Rifle Association of America, June 15, 1921

Dale Jones was a combination of Jesse James and Clyde Barrow, a Missouri bad boy with a winning personality who grew into a killer and whose lover joined him in a bloody death during a shootout with cops.

Jones was nowhere near the legend that either James or Barrow became, however, largely because his timing was bad for gaining national notoriety. He came along just as dime novels, which had turned nineteenth-century outlaws such as James into folk heroes, were dying out and before the emergence of the FBI, which did the same for Barrow and other gangsters.

For the law-abiding citizens of Kansas City and the surrounding region, Jones's timing was horrible as well.

The Missouri State Penitentiary discharged Jones on August 23, 1917, just months after Albert Pagel gained his release from the Leavenworth federal penitentiary. At about the same time, Frank Lewis was recruiting gang members after his brothers Ora and Roy had been sent up on life sentences for the murder a St. Louis policeman, breaking up the region's most bloodthirsty band of criminals.

Jones had served eighteen months of a two-year sentence for grand larceny related to a car theft three years earlier. Considering what he had done — and what he was suspected of having done — in the years before his conviction, Jones might have been laughing during his entire stay in the pen.

By the time Missouri law enforcement caught up with him in January 1916 — and finally held on to him — Jones had been connected to the murders of a police officer in Kansas City and a constable in Butler, Missouri; was arrested at least five times for car theft, as well as on assorted other charges; had escaped custody three times (including once when a fellow inmate who joined him wound up dead under suspicious circumstances); had attempted to escape custody many more times; had threatened to blow up a jail to free an accomplice who had been caught; and had threatened to kidnap the children of the Missouri penitentiary warden to free that same accomplice.

All this before his twenty-first birthday.

Jones's precise age is unclear. Several sources, including Missouri penitentiary records, say he was born in 1898 (that would have made him sixteen or seventeen when he entered that institution). Some newspaper articles pegged his birth as early as 1895.

However young he was, he evidently looked even younger.

Jones was described as about five feet ten inches and 140 pounds with a fair complexion, light hair, blue eyes, small hands, and delicate features, all of which gave him two advantages over most gangsters. In addition to possessing the appearance of an innocent boy — an image he exploited in his encounters with authority figures — he also was able to successfully pose as a girl and, later, as a woman.

* * *

Beyond his female alter ego, Jones led an actual double life. As he became a bad boy legend in Missouri, he did the same in California.

While law enforcement in Kansas City and the surrounding region tracked, arrested, and rearrested Dale Jones, their counterparts in Los Angeles tracked, arrested, and rearrested Charles Forbes. That went on for more than two years before anybody in either city realized Dale Jones and Charles Forbes were the same youthful lawbreaker.

The first newspaper article to mention Jones, the *Holt County Sentinel* in August 1913, said that Jones's parents had divorced and that he was living with his father in Kansas City. It was there that police officer William Koger was killed in November 1913.

Two days later, Jones — probably no more than sixteen years old — was arrested for the murder in Hume, Missouri. With the assistance of John Shead, who had been his partner in crime for several years, he escaped while being transported by train to the Bates County Jail in Butler, Missouri. To free Jones, Shead shot and killed constable Sam Queen.

At that point, Jones's father bought a train ticket for his fugitive son and sent him to Los Angeles, where relatives lived.

Dale Jones, aka Charles Forbes, wasn't in California long — barely three months — but he managed to get arrested at least once on a car-theft charge. Los Angeles juvenile authorities let him go on probation.

By March 1914, Shead had been arrested for Queen's murder, so Jones returned to Butler, Missouri, determined to bust his buddy out of jail. He dressed as a woman to scout the situation.

Before he could act, however, four detectives in Kansas City grabbed him, then found in the room where he was staying a dress as well as an unmailed letter Jones had written to Shead's brother. It read in part: "John got me out when they had me for the Koger killing, and I'm going to get him out if I have to blow the … jail to pieces. I've got it all fixed. I'm going to blow the walls up and get John out."

Kansas City police sent Jones back to Butler, but not before thwarting his late-night attempt to escape from police headquarters by using an iron bar from his cot to pry loose the bars on his cell window. He had detached one bar and was working on a second before jailers intervened.

The jailers in Butler managed to hang onto Jones — who was facing only that car-theft charge — for a few months. Meanwhile, Shead was convicted of murder in June and sentenced to life at the Missouri penitentiary.

Still in the Bates County Jail in Butler, Jones plotted yet another escape. For this one, his accomplice was one George Johnson, an unfortunate soul if there ever was one.

The *Los Angeles Times* said that Johnson, who was about a year older than Jones, was "afflicted with an offensive disease" and that the jail's other occupants refused to stay in the same cell with him. Johnson, who was being held for a minor crime and would have been released the next day, agreed to help Jones escape on November 12, 1914.

Again using an iron bar from his bunk, Jones broke the cell door lock before he and Johnson dug a hole through a second-floor brick wall, fashioned blankets into a rope to lower themselves to the ground, and ran to freedom at about three in the morning.

Jones later said Johnson had been too fat to fit through the hole they had dug in the wall, so he left his cellmate behind and had no idea what eventually happened to Johnson. True or not, that story didn't emerge until after Johnson's fate had become news.

Two days after the jail break, a hunter found Johnson's bruised and battered body in Miami Creek near a railroad bridge about five miles south of Butler.

Among the theories: Johnson died after being hit by a train that knocked him into the creek below; he was attempting to board a train when he fell; he sat on the bridge, dozed off, and tumbled from the bridge; or he had annoyed Dale Jones so much that Jones killed him. A coroner's jury ruled that Johnson "came to his death by causes unknown."

We know exactly what happened to Jones — he took off for California again.

* * *

On November 17, 1914, just five days after his escape from jail in Missouri, Charles Forbes was arrested for car theft in Los Angeles, drawing a sentence of six months at the Whittier Reform School.

Forbes, also known in LA as Ford Engles and Loyd Rexall, apparently spent much of the next fourteen months at Whittier serving that sentence and another one for a car theft committed in October 1915. While free between stints in Whittier, he was arrested in Long Beach, California, on several charges — including yet another car theft — but was released.

During his first stay at Whittier, he managed to get a message to a detective for the Missouri Pacific Railroad who was seeking him for his crimes in Missouri. Jones told the detective to pass along a message to D.C. McClung, warden of the Missouri penitentiary, which held Jones's buddy Shead at the time.

It read: "If it is the last thing on earth I do I'll kidnap one of the warden's children and demand the release of John Shead."

McClung had five children, ranging in age from eighteen months to twenty-one years.

If nothing else, Jones was persistent in trying to repay his debt to Shead for helping him escape in 1913. By the time Jones returned to Missouri, however, he was in no position to break Shead out of prison because he was heading there himself.

Missouri officials, no doubt with the help of that Missouri Pacific detective Jones had contacted, finally figured out that LA's Charles Forbes was their Dale Jones and tracked him down at Whittier in December 1915. But when the sheriff of Butler County in Missouri and an agent for the Missouri Pacific Railroad — armed with an extradition order from the Missouri governor — arrived to claim Jones, he didn't go willingly.

First, he claimed he had never set foot in Missouri. Then he fought extradition to Missouri, and he had powerful supporters in his corner.

Charles R. Burger, the California state chairman of the Prohibition Party, issued a statement saying Charles Forbes wasn't the desperate criminal his Missouri accusers claimed he was but was "a quiet, soft-spoken, modest, and courteous young man, admired and liked by all who come in contact with him."

As a capper, Burger called Kansas City "that cesspool of American political corruption" and said Missouri officials had wrongly accused Forbes of multiple crimes.

Meanwhile, Dr. Victor La Tour, described by the *Los Angeles Times* as a criminologist, testified that all of Forbes's criminal acts had resulted from the suggestions of others. La Tour claimed that Forbes was more susceptible to the influence of others than any other person he had met.

Just why Burger and La Tour took such an interest in the innocent-looking, fair-skinned teen from Missouri isn't clear. Regardless, the court wasn't buying what they were selling. It ordered Forbes to return to Missouri.

He was back in the Bates County Jail, as Dale Jones again, by January 11, 1916.

He was convicted on that grand larceny charge and sentenced to two years in the state penitentiary. *The Butler Weekly Times* said, "Jones was well satisfied with his sentence and thanked Judge Charles A. Calvird and the jury when the verdict was returned."

On February 24, 1916, he arrived at the state penitentiary in Jefferson City, where he reunited with his buddy John Shead and where he was soon joined by two other men he had criminal ties to: Ora and Roy Lewis, brothers of Frank Lewis.

Still a teenager, Jones no doubt got quite an education during his eighteen months in the big house. When he got out on August 23, 1917, he was a fully seasoned criminal. Within two months, on October 20, 1917, he returned to the state pen with Frank Lewis. They hoped to break out Ora Lewis, Roy Lewis, and John Shead but succeeded only in freeing Shead.

This was just as the United States' involvement in World War I was heating up. Rather than fighting their nation's enemies, however, Jones and the others waged battles of their own. They had few other options. They couldn't be drafted because they were felons. And their only real training was in criminal enterprises.

Jones and Frank Lewis formed a gang including Shead, Roscoe "Kansas City Blackie" Lancaster, and Roy Sherrill that left a trail of stolen cars, bank robberies, and dead cops across Missouri, Kansas, Oklahoma, Illinois, Indiana, and beyond.

In the ensuing thirteen months, their activities would be the stuff of criminal legend.

| 4 |

Albert Pagel

"So, into the maelstrom of Kansas City's wicked gaiety, at a period shortly before this country became involved in the World War, plunged beautiful young Mattie Howard, still an unsophisticated girl, but possessing a striking personality and a will to accomplish anything she set out to do. But she needed a dominating purpose or interest in life."

The Pathway of Mattie Howard (To and from Prison): True Story of the Regeneration of an Ex-Convict and Gangster Woman by M. Harris, copyright by Mattie Howard, 1937

Albert Pagel was a Secret Service man in Kansas City. At least that's what he told people.

But Mattie Howard knew better.

She probably also knew better than to accept thousands of dollars' worth of gifts from an ex-con who ventured away from Kansas

Albert Pagel
National Archives

City on extended "business trips" and returned with stacks of cash. But accept them she did.

Mattie didn't dive headfirst into the world of crime after joining Pagel in Kansas City in 1917. In fact, soon after settling into a room in a private home at 5222 St. John Avenue in northeast Kansas City, she held down two jobs, sorting mail orders in the office of the Montgomery Ward department store during the day and working the switchboard at the Bell Telephone Company in the evening.

"I was really making good in the big city," she said later. "My letters back home, sending money and a lot of news about my success, gave me the feeling that my mother now would feel I was right in leaving home."

But it wasn't long before she succumbed to the allure of the criminal underworld.

Albert treated Mattie to a lifestyle she had seen only in the silent movies, showering her with jewelry, perfume, and expensive hand-kerchiefs, and escorting her to restaurants, night clubs, and late-night parties. She developed a particular fondness for Chinese noodles.

Mattie, at her new lover's urging, also drank liquor for the first time. It started with one sip one evening, and before long she imbibed with the best of Kansas City's partying crowd.

The excitement of it all thrilled her. But the good times also took a toll, coming as they did after long days and nights working two jobs. Her letters home stopped. She arrived at Montgomery Ward's sleep-deprived and no doubt sometimes hungover, then dozed off on the job. Her concentration waned.

Mattie's boss at Montgomery Ward's told her she was no longer needed, and Bell Telephone soon fired her as well.

"With both my jobs gone, I did wonder what to do next," she said.

Then Albert called.

"Noting the strained tone in which I was talking, he soon found out I had lost both jobs. 'Don't worry, kid, I'll be right out.'"

Taking Mattie for a drive in his fancy car, Albert said she should find a new apartment and he would pay for it.

"When I protested about money, he laughed and took out a roll of money which my two hands could hardly span. He told me to shoot the wad; there was more where that came from. I stared in unbelief at the huge roll, and stammered I couldn't take it, only to have him tell me not to be a little silly."

Upon returning to her room, Mattie counted the bills in the roll. One thousand dollars.

She proceeded to rent a classy place in the new Ardmore Apartments at Eleventh and Forest. With Albert out of town — perhaps robbing a bank or stealing a car to be used in bootlegging — Mattie partied there with her friends from the telephone company.

She then went about spending her windfall, buying her first car — a used Maxwell — as well as new clothes, a dog, and a parrot. The entire thousand dollars was gone in eight days, and Mattie became the envy of her telephone company friends.

When Albert returned, Mattie expected him to be angry that she had spent all the money. Instead, he made her get rid of the car and the dog and replaced both with more expensive models.

"He laughed and called the car a pile of junk, sold it and bought me a Duesenberg, all upholstered in red leather and more gadgets on it than I ever learned what to do with."

Albert also provided Mattie with a new supply of cash, which went the way of the first batch.

"Furs, diamonds, lingerie, hats, everything I could think of. The apartment was furnished to the queen's taste, and if at times I had qualms of conscience, they were soon drowned in the whirl of good times with Al. Several times he left town, returning with huge sums of money which we threw to the winds like millionaires."

While Albert was on his out-of-town adventures, Mattie led a life of leisure. She spent much of her time with the girlfriends of Albert's cohorts. She had charge accounts at Kansas City's finest stores. According to *The Pathway of Mattie Howard,* she owned a $2,700 fur coat and a $500 mink cape and kept "as much as $20,000 pinned in her bosom."

Several months later, after Mattie's arrest, police detective Harry Arthur gave me the inside scoop on her relationship with Pagel. He said Mattie had opened a checking account at the Midwest National Bank on February 14, 1918, depositing $600. At that point, she still lived in a room on St. John Avenue. "While there she was frequented by a man named Albert Pagel, who, she said, was a 'Secret Service man,'" I wrote.

Arthur told me he had interviewed a woman who lived in the house on St. John Avenue and who knew Mattie.

"Miss Howard would often be away from home several days and nights," she said, according to Arthur. "I would ask where she had been. The girl would say she had been out on cabaret parties. She often would show me twenty-dollar and fifty-dollar bills. She said she had good friends who lent her money. No, Mattie was not working then. I remember once she told me she had a rich jeweler and pawnbroker downtown who loved her and wanted to marry her. No, she wouldn't tell me his name."

Mattie apparently wasn't yet directly involved in crimes. She lurked on the peripheries of the underworld, riding with Albert to meetings where the gangsters planned jobs while she waited in the car. She accompanied him on some out-of-town trips, but he insisted she not be seen with him at the hotels where they stayed, so they departed separately and met up later.

Meanwhile, Mattie spent every illicit dollar Albert gave her.

She also no doubt met the gangsters he associated with, including the notorious Dale Jones.

* * *

Before the first flowers bloomed in April 1918, everything changed for Mattie Howard.

As the Great War raged in Europe and the first sign of the devastating Spanish Flu epidemic appeared at Camp Funston, Kansas, about 125 miles west of Kansas City, she completed her metamorphosis from Catholic convent girl to outright gangster.

Her world began to turn one evening when Albert Pagel hastened back to Kansas City from a misadventure in the southwest part of the state, where Missouri borders both Kansas and Oklahoma. The area had been a haven for scofflaws for decades, dating to when what would become Oklahoma was Indian Territory. Oklahoma had earned statehood barely ten years earlier, in 1907.

Members of the Jones-Lewis gang were known to operate in that region, mostly stealing cars and robbing banks but also holding up fellow gangsters, taking bootleggers' cars and their illegal liquor. They were suspected of a unique ruse: Posing as agents for the Secret Service, they "arrested" bootleggers and then promised not to prosecute them if the bootleggers paid a fee.

Albert Pagel, remember, was known to impersonate a Secret Service man.

On an early spring evening in 1918, he burst into Mattie's apartment in a state of panic upon returning from southwest Missouri.

"Get your traps together and blow," he exclaimed. "Go to your mother's or anywhere till the heat is off."

Mattie asked if she had done something wrong, but Albert merely repeated his order to get packing and get going. When she refused, he grabbed her clothes, stuffed them into suitcases, and rushed her out the door.

Obviously, somebody was after Pagel. But why did he insist that Mattie get out of town?

Perhaps she knew too much about his illegal operations for him to risk her falling into the hands of the police. Or perhaps one or more of the bootleggers his crew had ripped off was on his trail and he feared for Mattie's safety.

In either case, as Albert put Mattie on a westbound train at Union Station, he told her to stay at her mother's house in Raton, New Mexico, until she heard from him. He would write in a few days when the coast was clear and tell her she could return to Kansas City

That was the plan, anyway.

No letter from Albert ever arrived, probably because he was in a jail cell in Springfield, Missouri, as of April 2.

Under the alias George M. Moore, Pagel had been arrested with J.A. Stanton (alias Jim Clancy) in northeast Oklahoma, where they were caught in possession of a car that had been stolen in Springfield.

He was returned to Springfield, where he was charged with burglary and larceny.

Of course, Mattie didn't know that.

When she arrived in Raton wearing jewels and expensive clothes, her mother spurned her, suggesting she was on the road to ruin. Mattie chafed, but she remained at her mother's house a few days. During her stay in northwest New Mexico, she crossed into Colorado to visit her sister and made a stop in Trinidad, Colorado. A restaurant operator there cashed her check on April 4, a seemingly innocent event that proved fateful for Mattie when the man recognized her several weeks later.

Receiving no word from Albert, she returned to Kansas City, where she searched for her lover, checking his usual haunts and tracking down his running mates. She heard Albert was in Tulsa, Oklahoma.

"So on to Tulsa I went, and looking up a man called Whitey in a pool hall, I asked for Al," Mattie would say later.

"I don't know him," Whitey said.

"Spying an English tweed coat belonging to Al hanging on the wall, I told Whitey I wanted the owner of that coat."

"Oh! Say kid, he's taking it on the lam. He's in Picher, laying low."

"So I went to Picher, Oklahoma, and finding the man Whitey had directed me to, he told me he had gone on to Miami, Oklahoma, with the officers hot on his trail. So on to Miami I went, arriving just twenty minutes after Al had been taken by the officers and rushed on a train for Springfield, Missouri."

The next stop for Mattie, then, was the Springfield jail, but she had problem: She didn't know what alias Albert was using when he was arrested. The jailer denied her initial request to see the man she said was her husband, saying no man by that name was housed there.

But after she described him, the jailer allowed her to see his prisoner, George M. Moore. Mattie visited with Moore/Pagel that day and returned the next day, when she offered her assistance.

"He slipped me a list of names to call on and try to get 'front' money, and mouthpiece, or attorney," she said. "Oklahomie, Blackie, Whitey,

Red, Dago Joe, and a lot of other names too far back in my mind to remember."

Mattie offered Paul M. O'Day, the prosecuting attorney in Springfield, whatever bond might be needed to free Pagel, but O'Day rebuffed her.

Albert told her to wait for him and if she "still cared for him, we were going to be married, so he said." She was still married to another man, so that would be a problem. And instead of simply waiting, Mattie continued her quest to free her lover, a mission she took to the extreme.

First, she retraced Albert's recent journey through northeast Oklahoma and southwest Missouri to retrieve his pistol, overcoat, clothes, and suitcase. She shipped them to his sister in Brooklyn. After hiring Albert a lawyer, she returned to Kansas City, where she retrieved the belongings she had left behind in her fancy new apartment and moved into the Sherman Hotel at Ninth and Locust.

Mattie also began seeking out Albert's criminal cohorts to request their assistance. That meant visiting some of the seedier parts of town to hook up with Dale Jones and others of his ilk.

* * *

At this point, it was mid-April 1918. Mattie was out of work, and her golden goose was cooked.

Perhaps it occurred to her that she could make money by following Albert's lead. Using his connections in the underworld, she could raise cash to pay for Albert's bond and his defense — and maybe to bribe a few officials.

One source of that cash was Sam Taylor. The thirty-seven-year-old bootlegger, burglar, and all-around criminal bungler, whom some reporters referred to as a "half-breed," had served in Leavenworth at the same time as Albert Pagel and Oliver Howard before being discharged November 16, 1917. He operated out of Picher — the town in the northeast corner of Oklahoma that Mattie had visited in searching for Pagel.

Taylor had spent most of the previous seven years in Leavenworth on five-year sentences for two different convictions, first in 1910 for a burglary in San Angelo, Texas, then for breaking into a post office in Oklahoma City in 1914.

It figures that he had known Pagel and Oliver Howard in Leavenworth and thus was familiar with Mattie. In any case, Taylor became Mattie's helper — if not her lover — just after Pagel entered the Springfield jail.

The Pathway of Mattie Howard said that Taylor had long "been fond" of Mattie and that once Pagel was locked up, he took advantage of the situation. I saw a different relationship, writing that Mattie "wheedled" money out of Taylor and sent it to Pagel. Mattie and Taylor then went together to Kansas City.

Perhaps it was a coincidence, but at the same time Mattie was looking desperately for cash, she befriended the wealthy Joe Morino in downtown Kansas City. Mattie's later accounts, unlike those that appeared in newspapers at the time, painted their relationship as totally innocent:

I used to eat my meals in the Victor Café, at Eighth and Grand, and right next door was the shop of Joseph Morino, called the "diamond broker." I wanted to take my mother and brother a little gift, so I stopped in the shop and bought some chip diamond earbobs and a signet ring. I wanted it engraved with his initials, and Joe told me to come back in a couple of days. I gave him a check for the amount, about twelve dollars, and went next door to eat. After I had eaten, I found I had only a few coppers in my purse and offered the cashier a check, which was refused. Morino and his wife were eating at another table, and he offered to cash my check, which I accepted gratefully. I can still see the little black book in which he tucked my check.

Mattie's movements for about a month are a mystery.

We know she checked out of her fancy digs at the Ardmore Apartments and registered at Kansas City's Sherman Hotel on April 15, 1918, after returning — presumably with Sam Taylor —from Springfield, where she had visited Albert Pagel in jail.

"Here she seemed to have plenty of money and often boasted that she had a wealthy diamond broker on the string, who was in love with her and wanted to marry her," I wrote in *The Star* about a year later.

She checked out of the Sherman on April 18, leaving a forwarding address of general delivery in Kansas City. Then, on May 18, she registered at a rooming house in Joplin, not far from Springfield and Pagel.

So where was Mattie Howard for those unaccounted thirty days?

The Sunday supplement stories published two to three years later suggested she had hooked up with the Dale Jones-Frank Lewis gang. Mattie needed money, so the partnership makes sense.

And we know the gang was busy during that time. In September 1918, Ghent, the acting police chief, said the Jones-Lewis gang had been responsible for some thirty holdups and bank robberies in the Kansas City area over the previous year. That didn't take into account the crimes the gang was suspected of in Kansas, southwest Missouri, and elsewhere.

In any event, Frank Lewis and the others operated without Jones for at least part of that period. Records show that on May 1, 1918, Dale D. Jones, age twenty-one, married Jewell M. Celano, twenty, in San Bernardino, California. Celano was also known as Margie or Marie Dean, and the marriage was a brief one.

Even without Jones, the gang had plenty of manpower — perhaps as many as twelve members. Two, Frank Lewis and Roy Sherrill, later provided police and prosecutors with details of its operation.

Lewis described a hierarchy that was hardly democratic.

"Jones and I never let these fellows like Sherrill and 'Blackie' (Lancaster) know anything," he said in September 1918. "When we wanted them for anything, we went and got them."

Sherrill, talking in November 1918, said, "Robbing banks was easy for us."

He described one such bank heist from about a year earlier.

"We had completed the job, secured the money, and were on our way back to Kansas City in motor cars when we met three autos loaded with Kansas City patrolmen speeding to the scene," Sherrill said. "I am satisfied the officers recognized us, but they never stopped."

Sherrill said the gang robbed a bank in Indianapolis and several banks on the outskirts of Kansas City. Jones or Lewis, who at 250 pounds was far more imposing than the boyish Jones, always directed the operations.

Sherrill was a fan of neither.

"Frank Lewis had a heart like a piece of rock," he said. "He said he had killed thirteen men, and I guess he told the truth."

Still, Sherrill preferred Lewis to Jones.

"There is only one man I want to kill, and that is Dale Jones," he said. "I hope I shall live to have that desire granted. There was never a gang of bandits organized but what had some honor among them, but I want to say there was no honor among the Lewis gang."

Lewis, meanwhile, blamed Sherrill and Jones for most of the gang's violence, saying, "I never killed a man — or a copper — in my life. But Dale Jones really is a bad boy, gents.

"Dale Jones won't be pinched. He took a vow he'd never be captured alive. He'll keep his word."

| 5 |

Joe Morino

"I did not kill Joe Morino. Such a thing would have never been done by me."
Mattie Howard, *The Kansas City Star*, February 23, 1933

J oe Morino personified the American dream.

Born in 1863 in Monastero Bormida, a tiny town in northwest Italy known mostly for a castle dating to the eleventh century, Morino set off for the United States in 1886, a time when tens of thousands of Italians immigrated to the United States each year.

He soon settled at the eastern edge of the Wild West — Kansas City, Missouri — a bustling cowtown, with its population exploding from 56,000 in 1880 to 133,000 in 1890.

When Morino arrived at the age of twenty-two, the city wasn't as wild and woolly as it had been a decade earlier, when the James-Younger Gang terrorized the region. Jesse James had been killed in nearby St. Joseph in 1882, and most of his running mates were either dead or in prison.

But Kansas City still had plenty of rough edges. A March 1884 story in *The Star* described a "gang of hoodlums and vicious vagabonds" that was menacing the city. A January 1888 story addressed a scourge

47

of robberies and killings, saying it might be the beginning of a "reign of terror."

Soon after arriving in his new hometown, Morino married Catherine Lavin, a Canadian. The couple, who had no children, eventually lived in a house well south of downtown at 822 West 39th Street.

The 1892 city directory listed Morino as operating a second-hand store at 922 Union Avenue in Kansas City's wide-open West Bottoms, situated in the valley where the Missouri and Kansas rivers meet. Morino's store was mere blocks east of what was known as the "Wettest Block in the World," a stretch on Ninth Street — near the state line with the dry state of Kansas — where twenty-four of the twenty-five buildings housed saloons.

An 1895 story in *The Star* described an incident that illustrated life in late-nineteenth century Kansas City.

A man named C.F. Robinson purchased a silver watch in Morino's store, but he returned within a few hours wanting to return it and claiming Morino had cheated him.

When Morino refused, Robinson decided to buy a revolver from the shopkeeper, who gladly made another sale. But then Robinson loaded the gun, shoved it under Morino's nose, and demanded the money he paid for the watch.

Thinking quickly — and taking advantage of his customer's apparent lack of common sense — Morino persuaded Robinson to wait in the store while he purportedly left to get a twenty-dollar bill changed. When Morino returned, he was accompanied by a police officer, who arrested Robinson on a robbery charge.

Diamonds eventually became Morino's special interest. He had his own pawnshop and jewelry store at 1201½ Grand Avenue in downtown Kansas City by just after the turn of the century. He later moved a few blocks to 812 Grand Avenue.

Morino, who had earned his U.S. citizenship in 1895, was becoming a wealthy man. *The Star* carried a small story in June 1914 about a five-month adventure Morino (evidently without his wife) took to

South America, where he climbed the Andes, and to Europe, where he visited relatives.

Morino also had at least two run-ins with the law. In 1903, he was fined fifty dollars for failing to report a watch he had pawned in his shop. He was fined fifty dollars again in 1917 for failing to report the purchase of diamonds, which also happened to have been reported stolen.

In the latter case, Judge Fred W. Coon declared of Morino: "I know you well. When I was young, I used to pawn my watch at your place, and you charged big interest, too."

The early years of the twentieth century, it's worth noting, were the peak period for the operations in Kansas City of the criminal element known as the Black Hand. Before the emergence of the Mafia, Black Hand operatives extorted — and occasionally murdered — fellow Italians, small-business owners in particular.

One of the Black Hand's regular targets, fruit importer and peddler Frank Carramusa, evidently fell behind in his extortion payments, and on March 28, 1919, he paid dearly. A shotgun blast killed his eleven-year-old son, Frank Carramusa Jr., in front of a crowd that had gathered in the street after a car accident. Paul Catanzaro, a known Black Hander, was identified as the shooter and eventually arrested, but he was never convicted because witnesses were afraid to speak up.

Clearly, Morino and his pawnshop/jewelry store would have been an inviting target for the Black Hand.

The diamond king also had another potential weakness.

"Morino is said to have been particularly susceptible to blond women," a story in *The Post* said, "friends saying that it had come to their knowledge that persons desiring to sell diamonds to him often employed blond women, knowing that Morino would pay these women more for the diamonds than any one else."

At five feet four inches and 170 pounds, Morino didn't overwhelm women with his physical presence. But his diamonds were a different matter. He was known to wear them in addition to selling them.

In the end, that might have gotten him killed.

Touraine Apartment Hotel, 1412 Central Avenue, Kansas City
Kansas City 1940 Tax Assessment Photographs

* * *

Ira Allen, a porter and general utility man at the Touraine Apartment Hotel in downtown Kansas City, was going about his duties on the morning of Saturday, May 25, 1918. That meant knocking on doors and collecting trash, just as he did every morning.

The three-story Touraine, at 1412 Central Avenue, had opened barely two years earlier and included fifty furnished apartments, each with a living room/bedroom, kitchenette, and bathroom. An ad in *The Star* boasted of its "disappearing beds throughout" and "large beautiful lobby and veranda on first floor." It indicated the rates were nine to eleven dollars for a week and thirty-five to forty-five dollars for a month.

When Allen reached the top floor at about 10 a.m. that Saturday, he knocked on the door of 301 and received no response. He decided to enter the room with his pass key.

The decision turned him into a key figure in what *The Journal* called "the most brutal (murder) that has occurred in Kansas City for years."

Typically, Allen left the outer door open while he performed his duties in the three-room apartment, but this time he closed the door after entering. That afforded a view down an inner hallway toward the kitchenette and bathroom.

It was there that he saw the body of a fully dressed man, complete with a necktie, lying face up on the floor, his head extending into the bathroom and his legs stretched along the inner hallway floor. A man's hat lay on the floor near the body.

Drawing closer, Allen saw that blood covered the man's shirt front as well as a folded bathmat that cushioned his head. One towel covered his face, and another was wrapped around his right wrist, with a strand of bailing wire wound tightly over it.

Allen shook the body and realized the man was dead.

Glancing into the main room of the apartment, the living room/ bedroom, Allen saw overturned chairs, a table and dresser jammed against the wall, and blood splattered on the floor, chairs, and walls.

He notified the housekeeper, Corine Fleming, who telephoned authorities after surveying the carnage.

Police officers and deputy coroner J.S. Snider soon arrived, and Fleming escorted them to the bloody scene. Joining the investigators inside Apartment 301, Fleming stumbled over an object on the inner hall floor. She picked it up and handed it to a policeman.

The item was a blackjack, a relatively small hand weapon usually made of leather and filled with dense material. It was ripped open, and its contents, small buckshot and grains of wheat, were scattered on the floor. It also carried an aroma of women's perfume.

When police pulled open the disappearing bed, which had been closed and folded into a closet, they saw it was stained with blood.

Near the doorway leading from the living room/bedroom, they discovered a blood-stained thumb print above a button that allowed tenants to summon the front desk. Nearby was a light fixture on the wall that was bent in a way that suggested it had been pulled down during a struggle.

Police also found a man's size-sixteen collar, covered with blood, on a dresser in the apartment. Other evidence at the scene: an empty whiskey bottle, two hairpins, and a bottle of medicine bearing the label of a drug firm in Houston, Texas.

The housekeeper wasn't the only civilian trampling on the crime scene. I was there, as were other reporters. We took advantage of our firsthand viewing to describe the gore in detail for our readers. *The Post* even carried a crude drawing and diagram of the apartment's three rooms, complete with notations marking "bloodstains on wall" and "blood spot where body of victim was found."

By Saturday afternoon, just a few hours after the body was found, *The Star* and *The Post* ran front-page stories about the murder and identified the victim as Joe Morino — a "rich diamond broker" and "extremely wealthy." The stories said he had been beaten to death with a blackjack.

Over the next several days, Snider and the police provided facts as well as theories, conjecture, and opinions, and we ran wild with them.

* * *

Police arrested Allen, but they didn't suspect him of killing Morino. He was taken to the Nineteenth Street Station and held briefly when he supposedly refused to answer questions from Dr. Snider.

Within three weeks, Allen not only was answering questions, he had become the most important witness in the arrest of the person the police decided to pin Joe Morino's murder on.

In the meantime, Morino's battered corpse had been taken to the Quick & Tobin undertaking business, where we newspapermen found his distraught, sobbing widow.

"It is terrible," Catherine Morino said. "My poor, dear husband. He was so good and kind to me. No, he didn't stay away nights — much. No, I never suspected another woman — we had been married thirty years. Wednesday night we went to a theater. I visited him in his store Thursday afternoon. That was the last time I saw him until..."

Snider determined that Morino's skull had been fractured over the left eye, causing a cerebral hemorrhage. He realized early in the investigation that the broken blackjack, which had no blood on it, could not have been the murder weapon and that the death blows were delivered by a harder object, perhaps the butt of a revolver. But the police never found the actual murder weapon.

The deputy coroner said that the bailing wire twisted around Morino's wrist suggested he had been bound to the bed or some other object but had managed to free his arm and escape into the hallway of the apartment, where he was overtaken by the killer or killers.

Given the perfumed blackjack, the hairpins, and the seemingly humane gesture of cushioning Morino's head, police surmised that at least one woman was involved in the killing. I wrote a story suggesting that two women murdered Morino, basing my conclusion on the conjecture of Snider and the police. In retrospect, my theorizing was not my best moment:

"The women demanded money, plenty of it. Morino protested in vain. Wasn't he worth almost ¼ million dollars? The women wanted a check, signed by him and made payable to bearer. They would keep the diamond broker prisoner until the check was cashed.

"Morino squirmed and managed to free his left arm. One of the women struck him on the head with a cheap 'blackjack.' The weapon was old and it parted at the end, sending a shower of small shot over the bed clothing. Stunned, Morino staggered to his feet. He was struck again and again."

The police had evidence to back the two-woman theory. A milkman reported seeing two women, one a blond, near a stairway at the Touraine at about 4 a.m. Saturday. He wondered what they were doing at that hour and why they appeared to be leaving the hotel by the back way.

Police eventually decided at least one man was involved, deducting that the death blows were too forceful for a woman to have delivered them. Another clue supporting that conclusion was the bloody size-16 collar found at the scene. Friends of Morino said he wore a size-15.

Police Lieutenant James J. O'Rourke said he believed Morino was attacked by two women with the assistance of a man hidden in the apartment. Another theory was that the killers were a woman with a man dressed as a woman.

* * *

Touraine employees said that three days before his body was found, Morino had checked in with a big blond woman, although hotel manager Walter Geraughty said he could not positively identify Morino as the man in question.

Geraughty was on duty at about 2 p.m. Wednesday, May 22, 1918, when a man carrying a black suitcase entered the lobby just ahead of a young woman dressed in a black skirt, white silk top, and a light straw hat. The man asked to be shown a kitchenette apartment, indicating he and his wife wanted it for a week.

Geraughty and Allen escorted the pair to Apartment 301.

"What do you think of the spot, dear?" the woman asked when they saw the room.

"You're the one to be pleased," the man replied.

"It sure is all right with me," she said laughing.

The man left his suitcase in the apartment, and the four returned to the lobby desk, where the blond woman signed the register "B. Stanley and wife, Detroit" and paid a week's rent, twelve dollars.

As the couple left the hotel walking arm in arm, the woman said over her shoulder, "My husband and I will be back soon."

Despite Geraughty's uncertainty, police were convinced the man who checked in was Morino. Given that the pair registered as "B. Stanley and wife, Detroit," it might be significant that Mattie Howard had lived in Detroit just before moving to Kansas City a year earlier.

The police immediately began a search for the blond woman who checked into the Touraine with Morino. Snider, the deputy coroner, said she was the key to the crime.

"When that woman is arrested, the murder will be solved, as there is no doubt in my mind that she planned the whole affair," he said, without indicating how he could possibly determine such a thing from the physical evidence at the crime scene.

The days after Morino's murder thus became a bad time to be a blond in the Midwest.

A woman named Catherine Felts, described as "a large woman and a blond," showed up on the police blotter, so Kansas City Detective Paul Conrad decided to haul her into police headquarters. She provided an alibi for the dates in question.

Felts addressed reporters: "Do you think the blond-haired woman charged with committing this crime, with all the publicity given the case, still would have blond hair?"

Detectives decided to hang onto Felts anyway "in hopes that she may know something about the other big blond," one of them said. She was held for two days before being arraigned in municipal court on a charge of vagrancy, whereupon Judge John M. Kennedy reprimanded the police for bringing her before him.

"I can't try the Morino case here," he said. "Apparently, you have no evidence connecting this woman with the case, anyway. The prisoner is discharged."

Another member of the unofficial Big blonds Club was arrested in Tulsa, Oklahoma. Police found a diamond brooch and several diamond rings in her possession, as well as clippings from Kansas City newspapers telling of the Morino murder. She admitted to formerly running a rooming house in Kansas City as well as to being in the Kansas City area the weekend of the Morino murder.

Again, police decided she was the wrong blond, and again they suggested she might know the other blond who went to the Touraine apartments with Morino.

* * *

Orla Puckett, the night clerk at the Touraine, had provided the police with what appeared to be another key piece of evidence. I quoted him in *The Star*:

"Just before seven o'clock last night, the man I know as 'Mr. Stanley' came into the lobby of the hotel with the woman I knew as his wife. And there was another woman with them, middle-aged, heavy set, and full-faced. They all seemed in a quiet frame of mind. Stanley took his key and with the two women went to 301. That was the last I saw of them. I don't know when or how the women left the hotel."

The "last night" in question, when Puckett saw Morino and the two women in the Touraine's lobby, had been Friday night, less than twenty-four hours before he made the statement to me and other reporters. You'd think a person would be clear about such a recent memory.

But — with some urging from police — Puckett eventually changed his story, saying he might have seen "Mr. Stanley" and the two women on Thursday night. That timing fit much better into the police's theory of the crime, specifically that Mattie Howard was the mysterious blond who lured Morino to his death.

As that theory developed, another significant element of the murder conveniently fell into place.

Snider originally declared that Morino had been killed late Friday night, some twelve hours before his body was found. But within a few days, the deputy coroner announced that the murder had taken place Thursday evening and that Morino had been dead more than forty hours when his body was discovered.

For that time of death to hold water, it meant that the two women (one a blond) whom the milkman encountered early Saturday morning were not involved in the crime and that Touraine employees had performed duties in the apartment several times Friday without noticing the corpse.

In addition, Corine Fleming, the housekeeper, said she entered the apartment at about 5:30 p.m. Friday and found two men putting up awnings in the main room of Apartment 301. She noticed no disarray and no sign the rooms had been occupied except that disappearing bed was down. The awning men, who evidently also didn't see the bloody corpse, finished their work about 7 p.m., received their pay, and departed.

Snider and the police insisted that the Touraine employees did not see Morino's corpse because it was concealed by the open door from the hallway. They hadn't closed that door, as porter Ira Allen did Saturday morning when he discovered the murder. But that didn't explain how the Touraine employees could have missed the blood on the walls and the general disarray in the apartment.

Other details indicated that the murder might have occurred Thursday night, however, especially that no friends or family members saw Morino or heard from him all day Friday or Friday evening.

There also was M.D. Duval. He was staying in the apartment adjoining 301 and said he heard a commotion between 8:30 and 9 p.m. Thursday that included the sounds of a man groaning and of furniture being thrown about. Duval did not report what he had heard Thursday night to the Touraine front desk, however, and he didn't tell anybody about it until several days later — after the murder became front-page news.

Meanwhile, *The Journal* reported just after the murder that a man in a second-floor apartment heard "what sounded to be a heavy thud" on the floor above him at about 10 p.m. Friday.

Despite the inconsistencies, Snider and the police stuck with their theory that the murder occurred Thursday, not Friday. Why? Probably because they knew Mattie Howard had an alibi for Friday night and not Thursday night.

Police didn't identify her as a suspect publicly for several days, but there is no doubt that they had zeroed in on Mattie within two days of the discovery of Morino's corpse.

She not only was blond, but she was known to associate with gangsters, so she had two strikes against her from the start. When police discovered a bad check for a hundred dollars from Mattie to Morino, she became suspect Number One.

Unfortunately, they didn't know where she was.

* * *

Zeffrino Gamba, who had been Morino's chief clerk for several years, provided police with most of the details that put them on Mattie's trail.

He said Morino met "the blond woman" in early April when she entered his store and bought jewelry worth $140, making a first payment of a hundred dollars with a check. The bank on which it was drawn returned the check to Morino with the notation "No account here." Morino hired a collection agency, which tracked the bad-check writer to the Sherman Hotel at Ninth and Locust streets.

Gamba made other claims about the woman in question.

He said that she had frequently called Morino and that Morino had told him of night meetings with the woman, complaining about the difficulty of getting away from his wife. He also confirmed that Morino had left the shop for about three hours Wednesday afternoon, precisely when "B. Stanley and wife, Detroit" checked into the Touraine, and said he suspected his boss was with the blond woman.

A major piece of evidence Gamba provided police was that the woman had called Morino on the telephone the night he was last seen alive at the shop, setting up a meeting near the Touraine.

Gamba said he answered the phone at about 8 p.m. Thursday, May 23, and recognized the woman's voice when she asked for "Joe." He overheard Morino tell her, "I'll meet you — yes — at Fourteenth and Central streets."

Morino closed the shop and left, and Gamba never saw him again.

When his employer didn't come to the store all day Friday or Saturday morning, Gamba grew worried because Morino never remained away so long without contacting him by telephone. Gamba immediately suspected foul play by the blond woman, even before news of Morino's murder became public. He eventually hired a private detective to work on the case.

Gamba's story — at least the version he told acting Kansas City Chief of Police J.L. Ghent — contained a detail that became lost as the case proceeded. He said the suspect was "a big blond woman, who is about thirty-five years old."

Mattie Howard was twenty-three.

***

Police investigators tracked Mattie's movements in mid-May to southern Missouri and northeast Oklahoma. She was still there as late as May 21, one day before "B. Stanley and wife, Detroit" rented the apartment at the Touraine. O.H. Stevens, a Kansas City pawnbroker, told police she had sent him a letter from Joplin asking about a necklace she had pawned with him and requesting it to be forwarded to Omaha. The letter was dated May 21.

Police also determined that Mattie had connected with bootlegger Sam Taylor in Picher, Oklahoma, and were tipped off that Mattie's mother lived in Raton, New Mexico. They were closing in on their blond suspect but still didn't know her whereabouts.

On June 6, 1918, Ghent issued a wanted poster for Mattie, complete with a $1,000 reward (reportedly paid for by friends of Morino), and distributed it to law-enforcement agencies around the country.

The police, who had previously withheld Mattie's name, indicated a state warrant charging murder had been filed against her. The circular included the following description of Mattie Howard: "Height 5-10, Weight 155 lbs., Blue Eyes, Perfect Blond Hair, Fair Complexion, Well Proportioned, Neat, and Dresses Very Fashionable. Lower Limbs Extremely Large."

| 6 |

Jesse E. James

"When I arrived in Kansas City, in custody of the officers, I found that Jesse James, the son of the notorious bandit, was to defend me. That man's name alone was enough to convict me."

Mattie Howard, *Linn County Budget-Gazette*, June 28, 1933

By June 22, 1918, when the oddly matched traveling party of accused murderers Mattie Howard and Sam Taylor, police detectives Harry Arthur and Denver Mitchell and hotel porter Ira Allen arrived at Union Station — where they likely encountered hundreds if not thousands of U.S. soldiers going to or returning from Europe — Mattie already was big news in Kansas City.

Not only had she been the subject of a well-publicized manhunt, but the governors of Missouri and Colorado had been involved in negotiations over her return to the Show-Me State for prosecution. After she was escorted to Kansas City's police headquarters, her questioning was handled not by detectives but by Ghent, the acting chief of police.

"I was placed in the jail at Kansas City and hounded for days," she said. "Why had I killed the man? What did I do with the diamonds I stole? How did he happen to have my check on his body? Did I know the proprietor of the restaurant called Victor's? And, all the while, the scare heads in the papers.

"For five days I was hounded and worried and questioned. Over and over again, the same silly things."

The day Mattie returned to Kansas City, a reporter for *The Post* got a look at the murder suspect for the first time but wasn't able to talk with her. *The Post* reported on June 23 that Theodore Fernkas, manager of the Victor Café, had identified Mattie. Fernkas told police he was certain she was the woman who was talking to Joe Morino after she had tried to cash a check in his establishment the week of his murder.

The Kansas City Post, June 23, 1918

The article, which was accompanied by the first photo of Mattie to appear in a Kansas City newspaper, went on to say:

"Mattie Howard doesn't fit the description of the woman given out by the police and employees at the hotel. At the time of the murder of Morino, his companion was described as a 'big, heavy-set blond,' about thirty-five years old. Now Mattie Howard is twenty-three years old, and although she is rather

tall, she is not large, nor heavy set. Her hair is decidedly light, but not decidedly blond. She is not pretty, and only fairly well dressed."

This was the rare newspaper reference that described Mattie as anything other than attractive. Of course, she probably wasn't at her best when *The Post* reporter saw her that day, having just disembarked from an overnight train trip after spending most of a week in the Trinidad, Colorado, jail.

Mattie said later of her first days in a Kansas City jail cell: "Was I a physical wreck? Well, pictures taken of me then made me look like a woman of fifty."

I had a leg up on the competition because I had interviewed Mattie on the train returning from Colorado. The next day, I gained access to her again after she had spent her first night in a cell at the police headquarters in downtown Kansas City.

As I approached, I heard her singing "There's a Long, Long Trail," a popular song from the ongoing Great War.

In a June 24 story, I wrote: "The words, sung in a clear soprano voice, resounded through the halls at police headquarters early yesterday morning, and even could be heard by persons passing along the street outside."

Nights are growing very lonely,
Days are very long;
I'm a-growing weary only
List'ning for your song.
There's a long, long trail a-winding
Into the land of my dreams,
Where the nightingales are singing
And the white moon beams.
There's a long, long night of waiting
Until my dreams all come true;

Till the day when I'll be going down
That long, long trail with you.

She was remarkably cheerful as she greeted me, sitting on her cot and showing no signs of nervousness. After telling me she had slept soundly, she responded with a smile when I asked whether she was worried.

"No, not in the least. I am innocent and have nothing to worry about," she said.

* * *

So, you've been arrested and charged with first-degree murder. You're 23 and essentially a stranger in town, having lived there less than a year, and you have few friends other than some telephone operators and a gaggle of gangsters.

What are you supposed to do?

Well, if you're Mattie Howard, you hire the son of America's most notorious outlaw to be your lawyer.

As bad an idea as that sounds from today's perspective, it was hardly remarkable in early twentieth-century Kansas City.

Jesse E. James, commonly known as Jesse James Jr., was a well-known defense lawyer in the city where in 1872 his father and Uncle Frank had robbed the Kansas City Industrial Exposition in front of an estimated ten thousand fairgoers.

Most Missourians considered the James boys more as heroes than as villains. But Jesse E. James still had to live down the family name, even in Kansas City. His mother, Zerelda, moved the family there after Robert Ford shot and killed Jesse James in 1882 in St. Joseph, Missouri, when the younger Jesse was six years old.

Young Jesse Jr. eventually became a fixture in the Jackson County Courthouse in Kansas City — but not as a defendant. In 1898, he opened a cigar stand in the building's lobby, where he made valuable connections with judges and lawyers.

Those connections came in handy later that year, when he was arrested after the robbery of a Missouri Pacific train in the Leeds area of Kansas City. The son of a bandit legend was acquitted during a trial the next year. Moreover, the leader of the gang that robbed the train, William W. Lowe, admitted in 1910 that he had lied when he testified that young Jesse James was involved.

By then, Jesse James Jr. was an established name in the Kansas City legal community.

He had used his profits from the cigar stand in 1901 to open a pawn shop and jewelry store at 1215½ Grand (just a few doors down from a similar shop operated at the same time by Joe Morino), and he continued running the shop while attending the Kansas City School of Law at night.

Upon graduating in 1906 at the age of thirty-one, James opened a practice in the Scarritt Building in downtown Kansas City.

"I shall never specialize in criminal practice," he said at the time. "There isn't enough money in that class of work. Few men who commit acts of violence have any money. The money is in corporation law and in will cases."

Jesse James Jr. did, however, venture into criminal law — and it did not go well.

The American Bar Association doesn't publicize win-loss records for trial lawyers, but if it did, James would have been the equivalent of the 1952 Pittsburgh Pirates. Based on coverage in newspapers — which presumably consisted of his biggest, most important criminal cases — James should have been sent back to the minor leagues.

In the years before Mattie hired him, James defended a nineteen-year-old man accused of killing his sweetheart (guilty; sentenced to nineteen years), a fifty-year-old man accused of robbing a jewelry store (guilty; fourteen years); and a seventy-year-old man accused of attacking a twelve-year-old girl after promising her candy and money (guilty, ten years).

Then there was the case of sixty-year-old Dr. C.A. Trautman and thirty-five-year-old Florence Clifford, who admitted they lived as man and wife in Kansas City even though Dr. Trautman had a wife and three children in St. Louis. They were sentenced to six months in jail, then resumed their cohabitation.

After relatives of Clifford complained to police, the loving couple returned to court on vagrancy charges. They told Judge Edward J. Fleming they had continued living together on the advice of their lawyer, Jesse James Jr.

"Did you give your clients that advice?" Judge Fleming asked James.

"Certainly," James replied.

Dr. Trautman then interjected, "I do whatever my attorney says."

"So do I," Clifford added.

"Doctor, would you jump from a bridge if your attorney advised?" Judge Fleming queried.

"Well, er, no, I don't believe so," Dr. Trautman said.

He and his honey were fined $200 each.

Jesse James Jr.'s practice before 1918 consisted primarily of personal-injury lawsuits, some of which he no doubt won. By June 1918 when Mattie hired him, however, James had lost every criminal case that the local newspapers covered.

Actually, it is likely that Dale Jones or another of Mattie's gangster friends hired James, who had become the go-to mouthpiece for Kansas City's underworld characters — at least until his remarkable incompetence became obvious to anybody who was paying attention.

In the months after Mattie hired him, *The Star* covered five other murder cases in which James was the defense lawyer. All went to trial within a five-month period.

In one case, James presented an insanity defense. In another, he called only two witnesses. In the other three, he called no defense witnesses at all.

All five defendants were found guilty and sentenced to life in the Missouri State Penitentiary.

None of those cases rivaled Mattie Howard's for notoriety. It generated by far the most publicity of any case in James's career, and even with the Great War raging in Europe and the influenza pandemic claiming millions of victims worldwide, Kansas City newspapers kept Mattie and Jesse James Jr. in the news for months.

* * *

Two days after returning to Kansas City as a murder suspect, Mattie was paraded in front of several witnesses, including Walter Geraughty, manager of the Touraine Apartment Hotel. They all identified her as the blond whom police had been seeking in connection with the murder of Joe Morino.

When Geraughty pointed his finger at Mattie and said he was positive she was the woman, she responded with a smile and said she had never been in the Touraine. Far from being upset with her circumstances, she joked with police officers, describing her situation as "just like a movie stunt" and saying her whereabouts the week of the murder was "for me to know and you to find out."

Then Ghent took over.

The acting chief of police questioned Mattie for three hours, trying to tie her to Morino, the Touraine, and the murder. She never cracked, although she admitted, "It looks bad for me."

I provided an eye-witness account in *The Star*:

"During the severe cross questioning, the expression on her face never changed. She answered each question slowly. Several times she contradicted herself, but stoutly denied she knew anything of how Morino was murdered or that she even went to the Touraine Apartment Hotel with him."

Mattie, accompanied by Jesse James Jr. and another lawyer, Ira McLauglin, smiled throughout Ghent's grilling.

"Since I have a perfect alibi, Chief, I guess I had just as well tell you where I was the last week of May," Mattie said. "I was in Tulsa, Oklahoma. I stayed at a hotel just a block and a half from the depot, but I don't know its name. It was above a clothing store and can be found easily. I registered under the name of Mrs. George Moore. The register will show that name in my handwriting."

Mattie refused to give Ghent a sample of her handwriting, and he eventually gave up his efforts to elicit a confession from his young suspect. He ordered her back to her cell.

"She seemed to be none the worse off for the three hours of questioning, and asked for something to eat," I reported. "She ate heartily."

Despite his suspect's denials, by the end of the day Ghent was convinced Mattie was guilty.

"I have no doubt that she is the right woman," he said. "I have asked her if she was in Kansas City at the time of the murder, and she first admitted that she was and later said she was in Oklahoma. I also asked her if she knew Morino. She said she knew him slightly, but that she never met him any place except the store. She also admitted that she gave Morino several checks but denied that any of them were worthless. I believe she will make a confession in a few days."

The confession never came.

* * *

June 24, 1918, was a busy day for Mattie Howard and Jesse James Jr.

In the morning, they requested and received a temporary restraining order from Judge W.O. Thomas of the circuit court to prevent the police from taking measurements, fingerprints, or photographs of Mattie. James said the order was the first of its kind issued in Kansas City and was based on a New York murder case.

That court appearance was largely a sideshow because it turned out the police already had taken Mattie's measurements, fingerprints, and photographs. A few days later, however, the state Supreme Court issued an order restraining the police from taking more photographs and fingerprints, from placing her photograph in the rogues' gallery, and from sending her fingerprints to other police departments.

The court also ordered the police to allow Mattie's attorneys to confer with her privately, which James told the court the police had been preventing.

These were small victories for James, but victories nonetheless.

The afternoon of June 24 saw Mattie arraigned on a first-degree murder charge before justice of the peace Denny Simrall. She pleaded not guilty. Simrall set her bond at $50,000 and scheduled a preliminary hearing for July 6. Unable to pay the $50,000, Mattie landed in the Jackson County Jail to wait for her preliminary hearing.

Meanwhile, a development related to her case grabbed headlines.

On July 4, two Kansas City police detectives returned from Joplin, Missouri, where they had collected a married couple, George and Maude Milner, and charged them in the murder of Joe Morino. At about thirty-five years old, five feet five inches, and 180 pounds, the dark-haired Maude Milner fit the description of the second woman (Mattie Howard supposedly being the other) seen with Morino at the Touraine shortly before his murder. She also admitted that she knew Mattie, Sam Taylor, and Albert Pagel (under his alias of George Moore) and that she was with Mattie in the days after Morino's murder. Plus, the detectives reported that the couple wore $2,000 worth of jewelry (the same amount reported missing from Morino's murdered body) when arrested.

Assistant prosecutor I.M. Lee questioned the Milners on July 5, and they evidently said something to convince him of their innocence. Lee immediately announced the state warrants containing the charges against the Milners would be dismissed at the preliminary hearing scheduled for July 6.

On that day, Simrall continued Mattie's preliminary hearing to July 16. He also reduced her bond to $20,000, which she still could not raise, and dismissed the charges against Sam Taylor, who was released.

That left Mattie as the only person on the hook for Morino's murder just two days after four people had faced charges.

* * *

Perhaps it was a coincidence, but in the days between Mattie's arraignment and her preliminary hearing — as she sat in the county jail because she couldn't come up with the $20,000 bond — Dale Jones and his gang perpetrated its boldest robbery.

Or maybe it wasn't a coincidence.

Jones might very well have been trying to raise funds to help Mattie. Even though he had recently been married, Jones was said to be sweet on Mattie, who for the baby-faced gangster was an older woman. It also was possible that Mattie had been covering for Jones throughout her encounters with the police and he believed he owed her a debt. Jones was a logical suspect in the Morino murder, but the police never publicly mentioned him in connection with the crime.

At the very least, Dale and Mattie shared a kinship in crime, which came with its rewards for those nabbed by the law.

Mattie later said that "through the grapevine of the underworld, the news spread that Mattie Howard was true to the code and was telling nothing. So, in repayment, funds were furnished to release me."

That release came less than two weeks after the Jones-Lewis gang pulled the bold train robbery that made news across the Midwest. It also ultimately led to the gang's demise.

Jones, Lewis, and others in their circle had been in Kansas City most of the spring and early summer. In fact, Jones and Roscoe "Kansas City Blackie" Lancaster were identified as the men who robbed a bank just outside Kansas City in Sugar Creek on May 25, the very day that Joe Morino's body was found in the Touraine.

That crime paled compared with the job the Jones-Lewis gang perpetrated on July 10, 1918.

It was a train robbery that seemed to be taken from the James gang's 1870s playbook — except the perpetrators sped from the scene in cars instead of on horses.

The Star reported that thirteen armed, masked men held up the southbound *Texas Special* of the Missouri, Kansas & Texas Railroad a mile south of Paola, Kansas, and about forty-seven miles southwest of Kansas City.

The gang boarded the train at about 10:30 p.m. when it stopped on a side track to allow another train to pass. The bandits uncoupled the engine and the mail and express cars, grabbing the loot and shooting two MKT employees and a woman passenger.

Jones and Lewis might not have realized that by robbing money and mail from a train and shooting three people, they would be pursued not just by local law enforcement officers (who couldn't chase them across state lines), but also by railroad, postal, and Pinkerton agents who could track them anywhere — and did.

They eventually caught up with Lewis in September, and he provided details on the MKT robbery. He said that he and his cohorts had been led to believe the train contained $250,000 and that five, not thirteen, gang members were involved — he, Jones, Roy Sherrill, Blackie Lancaster, and Earl King. They employed a clever ruse while communicating with each other.

"We used numbers so we would not shoot our own fellows," Lewis said. "… Sherrill called any number as high as thirteen to make the people believe that there were that many in the gang.

"I backed the engine and the two cars a half-mile to the road crossing and whistled twice for the other fellows to come on. I went into the field and got my car and loaded the strong box into it.

"We headed for Kansas City and got there about 1 o'clock in the morning."

Two posses totaling more than thirty men went after the gang but lost the trail, and the railroad, express company, and U.S. Postal Service offered a reward of $39,000 ($3,000 per alleged robber). But even with the Pinkertons soon joining in the hunt, they came up empty for more than a week.

When law-enforcement officers finally caught up with the train robbers, they were still in Kansas City.

Jackson County Marshal Harvey Hoffman and four Kansas City detectives, having learned that Dale Jones and Frank Lewis were staying in a nice residential neighborhood at 3715 Wyandotte Street, converged on the house during the early morning of July 18. All they found inside were two women, a sixteen-year-old girl, a ten-year-old girl, and an infant boy.

Their backup plan was to wait inside the house to see whether Jones and Lewis would show. They waited, and waited, and waited as the women grew more and more anxious, especially when the police refused to let them answer the phone when it rang.

Finally, at about 9:30 p.m., a high-powered Cadillac rumbled up to the house. One detective dashed outside and approached the car, which contained four men who put a spotlight on the detective and opened fire. Although blinded by the light, the officer raised two revolvers and returned fire. His cohorts in the house then joined the gun battle, but they couldn't prevent the Cadillac from speeding away.

No officers were injured, nor apparently were any of the occupants of the Cadillac.

After inspecting the contents of the house, which included $400 worth of the jewelry taken from the *Texas Special* as well as a derby hat believed to have been worn by one of the train bandits and bullets like the kind used in the holdup, Marshal Hoffman was convinced he had his men. Only he didn't really *have* them. Jones, Lewis, and friends had gotten away again.

* * *

Having come up empty in their search for their prime suspects, authorities decided to hang onto the people they did have. The women they arrested gave their names as Margie Dean and Fanny Rogers, and the girls as Bessie Clayton and Gertrude Rogers. The infant was John Clayton Jr., ten months old.

After the names and relationships were sorted, police realized they had a treasure trove of the bandits' loved ones:

Margie Dean was the wife of Dale Jones, who most recently had been going by the name Lloyd Dean.

Fanny Rogers was the mother-in-law of Frank Lewis. Bessie Clayton was Fanny Rogers's sixteen-year-old daughter; she was the new bride of twenty-six-year-old Frank Lewis, who had been using the alias Harry Clayton.

John Clayton Jr. was the newlyweds' son. Gertrude Rogers was Fanny's ten-year-old daughter.

The women told the police of their relationships to Jones and Dean but said little else. Newspapers, on the other hand, reported details of the bandits' recent escapades in Kansas City that made the police appear inept at best.

The stories indicated that in the days since the MKT holdup Lewis and Jones had been openly socializing around town without being recognized by police and that officers had seen Jones in saloons but never confronted him. In fact, Jones had spent much of one afternoon at the Woodland Avenue police station, where he brought a motorcycle to show a patrolman. The officer, who wound up buying the motorcycle, also went for a ride with Jones in that fancy Cadillac.

For his part, Lewis was said to have been stopped twice for speeding since the robbery, first paying a two-dollar fine in court and then forfeiting an eleven-dollar bond.

Finally, just two nights before the encounter at 3715 Wyandotte, a police car had stopped a vehicle containing some of the suspected robbers at Sixty-fifth Street and Wornall Road, whereupon the gangsters jumped from the vehicle and fired on the police before escaping the scene.

Given the brazenness of the behavior of Jones, Lewis, and the others, police took it seriously when a man identifying himself as Dale Jones called the night after the shootout at 3715 Wyandotte, threatening that gang members were preparing to storm police headquarters to rescue their women.

Police formed an emergency squad of officers armed with riot guns (probably 12-gauge shotguns) and stationed men around city hall. That didn't go well.

I was at police headquarters and reported the following:

"Capt. Peter McCosgrove, while instructing several new patrolmen how to operate the riot guns, accidentally discharged one of the weapons. A hole was torn in a table. One of the new officers barely escaped injury. ... A score of officers sped to the scene of the shooting in the belief the bandits had arrived."

They hadn't, and they never did.

The Jones and Lewis women and children — including ten-month-old John Clayton Jr. — soon were sent to the county jail, where they briefly served as Mattie's cellmates. On July 22, Fanny Rogers, ten-year-old Gertrude Rogers, and John Clayton Jr. were moved from the county jail on the order of U.S. Marshal William A. Sheldon, who said jail was not an appropriate place for children but declined to say where the woman and two children were taken.

Charges were filed against the women, who hired none other than Jesse James Jr. as their lawyer, but they were released after several more weeks in custody.

Shortly before the wives of Dale Jones and Frank Lewis and the others arrived at the county jail, Mattie had another visitor. Her mother, who had come from Raton, New Mexico, was allowed to visit Mattie's cell, where she prayed silently and preached to her wayward daughter about God still being on his throne.

Mattie wasn't buying it. She saw no signs at all that God was helping her.

* * *

But she did have Jesse James Jr. on her side.

Mattie's preliminary hearing stretched over more than a week in the courtroom of Justice of the Peace Denny Simrall, although proceedings took place on only three of those days.

On the opening day, in a court room crowded with female spectators, the state presented witnesses who identified Mattie as the woman who registered at the Touraine Apartment Hotel a few days before the body of Joe Morino was found there. Other witnesses testified that she had previous encounters with Morino.

Mattie, wearing a blue dress at the defendant's table, was the picture of apathy as she displayed the same worry-free attitude as over the previous weeks, from her arrest and police interrogations to her interviews with reporters.

"Mattie sat serenely through the din made by the spirited voices of the attorneys," I wrote. "Occasionally she would read a newspaper, then smile about the crowded courtroom when her glances met those of various city detectives."

Seated in the first row directly behind her was the murder victim's widow.

"Mattie Howard once turned her head and observed the sobbing woman in mourning. The accused woman yawned indifferently."

The attorneys were anything but indifferent.

James P. Aylward, a prominent local attorney who later would become Boss Tom Pendergast's right-hand man, had been hired by Morino's estate to prosecute Mattie. He and Jesse James Jr. clearly were not chums.

Their interactions became so heated that court attendants moved to the counsel table fearing the attorneys would come to blows. Among their interactions:

Aylward (referring to Mattie): "I dare you to put her on the stand and let her tell her story to the world."

James: "Bah!"

Aylward: "Bah yourself."

James: "Keep still, Jim, I don't need any help."

Aylward: "You'll need help before this case is over."

Aylward: "Put on testimony — you're four-flushing — camouflaging."

James: "No man in town has anything on you, Jim, when it comes to camouflaging."

James: "The Supreme Court has said in a recent case that you, Jim Aylward, and your partner, Frank Walsh, are hired as special prosecutors in cases, hired by private interests, who demand convictions regardless of their guilt or innocence. How about it, Jim?"

Aylward: "You give me credit for a great reputation, Jess."

The second day of the preliminary hearing, July 19, had fewer fireworks as Ora Puckett's testimony for the defense dominated. The night clerk at the Touraine swore that Mattie was not one of the two women who accompanied a man, thought to be Morino, up the Touraine's stairway shortly after 8 p.m. May 24, the night before Morino's body was discovered.

James contended that Morino was killed that night, a Friday, not the previous night as the prosecution insisted, so Puckett's testimony supported his theory in addition to indicating that Mattie wasn't the killer.

"I was behind the hotel desk," Puckett testified, "when a man, answering the description of Morino, and two women, one a blond and the other dark-haired, entered the hotel lobby from the street. The man started toward the room key rack, but the blond remarked, 'I have it,' and the man then rejoined the women. All walked upstairs.

"I had accounted for all the persons in the hotel but for this trio, so there was no doubt in my mind that they were the occupants of Kitchenette 301, which had been rented about noon the Wednesday before to a man and a woman registering as 'Mr. and Mrs. B. Stanley, Detroit.' I am positive neither of the women I saw that night was the woman I now see in the courtroom, Mattie Howard."

Puckett stuck to his story through a lengthy cross-examination.

The prosecution argued that Morino was dead by then anyway, so Puckett's recollections were irrelevant. Same for the testimony of milkman Orville Bailey. On July 23, the third and final day of the preliminary hearing, Bailey testified that he saw a blond and another woman near a stairway leading to the third floor of the Touraine at 4 a.m. May 25, just hours before the murder was discovered. He said neither woman was Mattie.

More crucial for the defense were witnesses who testified that they were in No. 301 on Friday, May 24, and did not see Morino's body, which made it hard to believe he had been killed the previous night.

On the other hand, the testimony of M.D. Duval, who occupied the apartment adjoining No. 301, supported the prosecution's time of death. He said he heard a ruckus in No. 301 on the evening of Thursday, May 23, including a noise that sounded like a chair falling and what seemed to be a groan.

All of which left the prosecution with a totally circumstantial case that caused Justice Simrall to have doubts about Mattie's guilt — but not enough doubts. He bound Mattie over for trial in Judge Ralph S. Latshaw's criminal court, setting her bond at $10,000.

"The outstanding bit of evidence that caused me to hold Mattie Howard for trial," Simrall said, "was the identification by Ira Allen, Negro porter, who swore Mattie Howard registered at the Touraine the Wednesday before the finding of the body Saturday. There is not a strong case, however, that the accused is guilty."

The next day, Latshaw set a trial date of October 7 and reduced the bond to $5,000, which Jesse James Jr. and a man named Denny Costello provided.

Mattie was out of jail, one day short of two months after the discovery of Joe Morino's dead body.

| 7 |

Jones-Lewis Gang

"Mattie Howard, the most picturesque woman crook known to police of the Middle West ... was in reality the siren of the underworld, for whose favor men dared death and murdered with a smile. Her softened glances lured them to destruction, and her mocking scorn drove them to hell."
The Kansas City Post, November 20, 1921

This is the point in the Mattie Howard story when she became the brains behind the Jones-Lewis gang's increasingly brazen activities. That's if you believe the Sunday supplement stories that came along a couple of years later:

"(She) forced hardened criminals to her will." *The Ogden Standard Examiner*

"Through her cool-headed foresight and genius for organization, the Jones gang became the most feared predatory band in the Southwest." *Atlanta Constitution*

"(She) queened it for ten years over the crime kings of the Middle West." *Buffalo Times*

Although the stories exaggerated, there's no doubt Mattie had a close connection with the Jones-Lewis gang.

She became acquainted with Dale Jones and Frank Lewis after she and her ex-con lover, Albert Pagel, arrived in Kansas City and Pagel resumed his outlaw ways. When Pagel was arrested, Jones was among those she asked to assist her lover, although it doesn't appear he did. When Mattie was arrested soon thereafter and charged in Joe Morino's murder, on the other hand, Jones was more than willing to offer his assistance.

In the weeks after she was released on bond on July 23, 1918, their relationship appears to have continued. It's worth noting that this occurred after Pagel finally pleaded guilty to grand larceny in Springfield, Missouri, and began a two-and-a-half-year sentence in the state penitentiary on August 14, 1918.

Mattie was supposedly restricted to the Kansas City area while free on bond. At the same time, law enforcement officials were convinced that Jones, Lewis, and friends also remained (for the most part) in town even after barely avoiding capture on July 18.

It might defy logic that the gangsters didn't get as far away from Kansas City as they could after that close call with the law at 3715 Wyandotte Street. But, according to one source, there was a good reason: Mattie Howard.

Dale Jones "was stuck on Mattie," an ex-con who drove for the gangster said later in 1918. "That's why he stayed around Kansas City so much. He wanted to be sure she got help. Dale didn't leave the city for his Colorado vacation until Mattie was 'sprung' from jail."

Much more on that "Colorado vacation" later.

My article about Jones's driver was a scoop for *The Star*, one I thought might wind up saving Mattie's bacon. But it didn't work out that way.

I called the guy a "stool pigeon," but the police described him as unidentified informant. He told detectives Harry Arthur and Harry Rozzelle the following tale:

Police were tailing Mattie after her release on bond and, acting on a tip, staked out a bungalow in the northeast area of Kansas City where a friend of hers lived. As four detectives hid in the darkness, a man and a woman approached from a nearby streetcar line and entered the bungalow.

Before long, the woman emerged from the house, and a detective followed her back to the streetcar line. Recognizing Mattie, he trailed her to the downtown hotel where she had been staying since her release from jail.

Meanwhile, the other detectives searched the bungalow and found it empty.

The informant said that the man with Mattie had been Dale Jones, that he had seen the detectives hiding outside the bungalow, and that he had been prepared to rescue Mattie if needed.

"On entering the house, he walked out the back door, then crawled through the side yard until he got under a big rose bush near the front porch," the informant told the detectives. "There he waited, ready to open fire if you guys started to pinch Mattie when she walked to the car line. Told me so himself."

That wasn't all.

The ex-con, who told the detectives that members of the Jones-Lewis gang hired his car occasionally while in Kansas City, said Jones frequently dressed in women's clothes when he and his wife rode around town. During one of these excursions, Jones confessed to killing Morino.

"I overheard Jones talking to Mrs. Jones about his part in the Morino killing," the informant said. "I told Jones the next day of what I heard him say, and he got mad and threatened to 'bump me off' if I told anyone. I knew he'd keep his word, too."

Jones never got the chance to bump off the informant. By the time the man ratted out Jones to the Kansas City detectives, the young gangster was dead.

* * *

As Jesse James Jr. and the Jackson County prosecutors traded continuances and other delays, Mattie wound up waiting fifteen months from her arraignment to the start of her murder trial.

They were a fateful fifteen months. The world witnessed several of the biggest developments of the early twentieth century — worldwide war and pandemic, ratification of the 18th Amendment banning alcohol in the United States, and Congress's passage of the 19th Amendment granting women the right to vote.

A lot happened in Mattie's orbit, as well — most of it related to crime and punishment. And death.

There was a lot of death.

We're not talking about the millions dying during the Spanish flu epidemic, which reached its nadir in late 1918, killing 248 souls in just one week in Kansas City. Nor the hundreds of thousands perishing in the Great War, which was winding down toward the armistice signing of November 11, 1918.

No, the deaths we're talking about struck closer to home for Mattie.

They became a big topic for the later Sunday supplement stories, which wrote that gangsters fell under the spell of Mattie and her icy eyes before encountering violent deaths. The deaths of men who knew Mattie were fact; the spells were the likely product of literary license.

The demise of multiple Jones-Lewis gang members, combined with a few convictions, wiped out the crew before the end of 1918. Its downfall can be traced directly to the fateful Kansas train robbery on July 10 that attracted the attention of federal agents and nearly got Dale Jones and Frank Lewis nabbed eight days later in that house at 3715 Wyandotte.

For most members of the Jones-Lewis gang, the end came within a few weeks of that close call in Kansas City.

Dale Jones, Frank Lewis, and their associates resurfaced briefly in Indiana. With federal law enforcement officers and Pinkerton agents on their trail, they robbed a bank in Indianapolis of $18,000 on August 8.

They used cash from the bank robbery to buy clothes in Quincy, Illinois, on August 10, before robbing a bank in Greeley, Kansas, on August 14, then stealing a Cadillac in Chillicothe, Missouri, on August 19.

Each time they returned to Kansas City. But then Dale Jones brought up his idea of a vacation.

Four of the five gang members involved in the MKT robbery — Jones, Lewis, Blackie Lancaster, and Roy Sherrill, but not Earl King — headed west, taking along Jones's wife and Lewis's wife and family. In Denver, they met up with Lewis's mother and stepfather.

Jackson County Marshal Harry Hoffman and postal inspectors had been tailing the two wives since their release from jail after the failed police stakeout at 3715 Wyandotte. The officers tipped off Colorado authorities to be on the watch for the wanted men and their wives.

Colorado Springs police officers caught up with gang members on the afternoon of September 13 at a gas station, where a shootout ensued. Dale Jones shot and killed Colorado Springs chief of detectives John Rowan, and a deputized civilian suffered bullet wounds to his eye, foot, and hand. The gangsters sped away.

Police soon found them at a house in Denver where Lewis's mother and stepfather were staying. The desperadoes did not give up easily, challenging police in running gun battles in and around Denver. When the smoke cleared, police said there had been five gunfights that had left two officers dead and four injured.

Among the gangsters, Lewis, Lancaster, and Sherrill were wounded. Police arrested Sherrill and Eva Lewis, Frank's sister, after one of the gun battles. Lewis managed to elude the police but was arrested the next day as he attempted to leave Denver in a taxicab.

Dale and Margie Jones escaped through police roadblocks, as did Roscoe "Kansas City Blackie" Lancaster.

Lewis spilled his guts to postal investigators after officials took him into custody, providing details on the MKT holdup and on the gang's operations. He told officers, "It was a mistake to leave Kansas City."

"Yes, we had a good time in Kansas City," he said. "We went to picture shows and were having a great life until this vacation. Dale and 'Kansas City Blackie' would sneak away together and rob banks. Before we started on that fool vacation trip to Colorado, Dale showed me a suitcase full of gold. He said there was thirty thousand 'Iron men.'"

So, guess where Dale Jones, Margie Jones, and Blackie Lancaster headed in their stolen 1917 Marmon after the bloody fiasco in Colorado, with those postal investigators still on their tails and police in virtually every state west of the Mississippi on the lookout for them?

Kansas City, of course.

The town was known to be friendly to desperadoes on the run, plus the wounded Lancaster had relatives there and plenty of friends as well — including Mattie Howard. In fact, Lancaster, like Jones, was rumored to be sweet on Mattie.

Lancaster took refuge in a house at 1904 Montgall Avenue, where the plan was for him to recuperate from the wounds he suffered in Colorado. His brother Warren, who had served time for robbery but hadn't been arrested since leaving the penitentiary in March 1916, had rented the place only days earlier.

Jones carried Lancaster into the house, bringing with them medicine, bandages, and medical instruments, and placed his cohort in a bed upstairs. Lancaster proceeded to doctor himself, fearing a real physician would call the police.

Neighbors said two young women frequented the Montgall house. One report indicated a blond visited regularly to deliver food.

With so much traffic in and out of the house, it's not surprising that the police were onto the hideout within a few days.

The Flora Avenue police station received a call on September 24 from what police described as an underworld figure who claimed "Dale Jones and a part of his gang" were at 1904 Montgall. Arriving at the address to check it out were four officers. Not exactly overkill, considering the carnage the gang had heaped on law enforcement two weeks earlier in Colorado.

Warren Lancaster greeted the officers at the door and, when asked who was upstairs, said, "You might go up and see if you want to."

That was how one of the longest and loudest shootouts in Kansas City history began.

When two officers climbed the steps and snooped around on the second floor, they were greeted by a volley of shots from Blackie

Lancaster's automatic pistol. The cops beat a hasty retreat and called for help, and several cars loaded with officers arrived outside the house.

Lancaster propped a mattress against a second-floor window and began blasting away with multiple weapons, firing so often that police believed multiple gangsters were waging war on them.

Meanwhile, a crowd estimated at three thousand curious souls gathered to witness the shootout, which filled the residential neighborhood with gunfire for nearly two hours. By the time Lancaster could shoot no more, he had wounded three police officers and a soldier.

When police entered the house, they found two automatic pistols, a rifle, and a pile of ammunition next to Lancaster, whom they thought to be dead. He wasn't.

"I was a game bird," he whispered. "I put up a game fight. I'm done, boys. It's your turn."

With the shooting halted, the spectators rushed up to the front door.

"Lynch him," one person shouted.

"Don't do it, he's dying," an officer responded.

The crowd made room for an ambulance that rushed Lancaster to General Hospital, where I watched as the gangster's life slipped away. With two bullet holes through his body, he struggled to breathe as he lay on a stretcher on the receiving ward floor while workers buzzed around him.

"I'm dying," he spat out. "I'm dying."

That didn't keep assistant Jackson County prosecutor Shannon C. Douglass Jr. from trying to obtain a statement from the gangster.

"What is your name?" Douglass asked.

"I'm Kansas City Blackie."

"Where are the rest of the bunch, Blackie?"

No response.

Later, the prosecutor asked: "Who's the leader of the gang, Blackie?"

"Dale Jones."

"Well, where is he now?"

"I don't know."

"When did he leave?"

"Night before last."

At that point, Douglass's questions were met with silence as Lancaster clutched his chest and squirmed. His breathing grew more labored.

I described the next moments in *The Star*:

"Renewed efforts were made to stop the flow of blood, but without avail. The bandit's chin quivered, and he clutched again at his clothing and the blanket that had been thrown over him.

"The struggles became still weaker, until, with a paroxysm of pain, they ceased.

"The intern in charge drew the blanket over the dead bandit and moved the stretcher away from the operating table."

With Lancaster dead, police turned to his brother for answers. They had arrested Warren Lancaster after he answered the door at 1904 Montgall and invited officers to Blackie's upstairs shooting gallery.

His wounded brother never left the house, Warren said, after he and Dale Jones carried Blackie to his bed. "And they never would have got him yesterday had he not been wounded. He would have shot himself out."

He said Jones had not been to the house since he visited Blackie at 1 a.m. three days before the shootout. Still, police believed Jones might have escaped just after the shooting started, so they searched Kansas City for him without success.

Reports indicated he and Margie, still driving the stolen Marmon, headed to Oklahoma and robbed a bank in McAlester.

Soon thereafter, gang member Earl King surfaced in St. Louis. Police arrested him on September 26 and sent him to Topeka, Kansas, where the wounded Frank Lewis and Roy Sherrill already were in custody. That left Jones as the only gang member from the MKT holdup who remained both alive and at large.

Within three weeks, Frank Lewis joined Blackie Lancaster as a deceased gang member, although he went considerably more peacefully.

Weakened by a bullet wound through a lung since the violent vacation to Colorado, Lewis fell easy prey to the Spanish flu while being held in the Shawnee County Jail on federal charges related to the MKT holdup. He died October 16, with the official cause of death being pneumonia.

Sherrill and King soon left Topeka as well, although they didn't go far. After pleading guilty in federal court to the mail-robbery charges, both were sentenced to twenty-five years in prison and entered Leavenworth on November 13.

Sherrill opened up to a reporter for *The Post* as he and King waited with federal officers in downtown Kansas City to catch an interurban electric railway car to Leavenworth. With Lewis dead and the gang in tatters, Sherrill — the son of a Baptist minister — played the victim.

"It's all over, and in a way I'm glad," he said. "I tried many times to break away from Lewis and his gang, but I was afraid.

"I am not a bad man. I just got in bad. As for me killing a man, that is something I never did."

He had especially harsh words for Frank Lewis.

"I remember once in Kansas City he hit an old man on the head with a hammer and then robbed him. The old man was lying there in his death agonies. 'Go give him another rap and finish him,' Lewis told me. I refused, so Lewis went back and calmly hit the dying man another blow. It made me sick."

With that tale, Sherrill was off to Leavenworth.

For those keeping score on the Jones-Lewis MKT crew, the tally at this point was two dead, two in federal prison, and Dale Jones still on the run.

* * *

Mattie, free on bond and still awaiting trial, kept a low profile as the Jones-Lewis gang disintegrated.

Dale Jones, meanwhile, made headlines from coast to coast.

As might be expected, he didn't stick around for the funerals of pals Blackie Lancaster and Frank Lewis or to visit Earl King and Roy Sherrill in Leavenworth.

Instead, Dale and Margie headed for the Los Angeles area, where Jones had spent much of his wayward youth under the name Charles

Forbes and where his wife grew up and had family. Turns out Margie's real name was Marie Celano, and according to the *Los Angeles Herald*, she had two other living husbands.

On October 16, the happy couple rented an isolated eight-room house in Sierra Madre, tucked in the foothills northeast of Los Angeles, with Jones using the name David Moorhead on the lease. Dale and Margie had arrived in California driving a stolen Cadillac roadster, having driven their stolen Marmon into a river.

Margie made the mistake of visiting friends near her former home in Glendale, where she was recognized. Within two weeks, a postal inspector, Pinkerton agents, and Los Angeles County Sheriff's deputies were tracking the Joneses, having learned where they were living — with other outlaws, the officers no doubt presumed.

Figuring the isolated house in the foothills was a veritable fortress, the officers devised a plan to catch Jones in a place he would be more vulnerable. They learned he frequented the White Oaks filling station at the corner of Foothill Boulevard and Double Drive (now Santa Anita Avenue) to fill up his Cadillac, and they staked out the place, with the Pinkerton agents and deputies swapping shifts.

After two weeks, Dale and Margie finally showed.

Two deputy sheriffs, William Anderson and George Van Vliet, were using a shed behind the filling station as cover on November 19, 1918, when the Cadillac roadster rambled up with Margie Jones behind the steering wheel and Dale Jones in the passenger seat.

The car rolled past the station and stopped, whereupon Dale exited and hid among some trees as he surveyed the scene to determine whether an ambush awaited them. He didn't spot the deputy sheriffs — or any other suspicious activity — and returned to the Cadillac.

After turning the car around, Margie steered it back to the front of the station and stopped again, allowing Dale to hop out. He entered the building, chatted with the clerk behind the counter, and paid for the gas he intended to buy. When he walked out the door, the clerk signaled to Anderson and Van Vliet, who sprang from their hiding places and confronted Jones.

"Throw up your hands!" they shouted

"You've got me!" Jones responded.

But as he raised his hands, Jones drew a German Lugar from a holster and a Smith & Wesson .38-caliber handgun from a hip pocket.

Anderson shot at Jones, and then all hell broke loose.

The young gangster could have attempted yet another escape in a criminal career filled with them. But instead of dashing for the Cadillac a few feet away with the engine running, he returned fire at Anderson.

Margie immediately came to his defense. She grabbed an automatic pistol from the car floor and fired at Van Vliet, hitting him with a shot in the chest that sent him to the ground.

Now alone in the battle with the gangsters, Anderson blasted away with a shotgun. Jones fell to the ground behind the still-running Cadillac as if he were wounded, and Margie fired at Anderson until her pistol was empty. She threw it down and snagged another weapon from inside the vehicle.

When she rose to fire at Anderson, he unloaded on her with his shotgun. The pellets struck Margie in her right temple and shoulder, killing her instantly.

Now Anderson, with only one cartridge in his shotgun, saw that Jones not only hadn't been wounded but had begun firing repeatedly at him. The deputy stepped away from the cover of the building, leveled his shotgun at Jones, and pulled the trigger.

His shot found its target — Jones's head. The young bandit had finally met his match.

As Dale Jones gasped his final breaths, the Cadillac, with the dead body of his wife behind the steering wheel, rolled away from the filling station and into a ditch.

The *Los Angeles Times* reported that Margie Jones "met death with a defiant smile on her face," describing her as "far from comely" with "jet black hair hung loosely over her shoulders."

Her victim, the deputy sheriff Van Vliet, was rushed to a nearby hospital with blood gushing from a wound just above his heart and died four hours later. A soldier named Albert Brock, who had been waiting for a ride to Los Angeles, was found unconscious in the grass some twenty-five yards from the filling station, having been struck in the back by a stray bullet. His injury proved not to be life-threatening.

Also escaping with his life was Anderson. The deputy, who had fired the shots that killed both Joneses, later discovered two bullet holes through his coat, one within two inches of his heart.

In the days after the deadly shootout, law-enforcement officers entered the Joneses' rented house in the foothills near Sierra Madre and found thirteen revolvers, two rifles, and a stockpile of ammunition. Police proceeded to accuse Dale and Margie of being morphine users and of perpetrating various unsolved crimes in the area, including the murder of a wealthy broker. Nothing came of the allegations.

Meanwhile, a rumor spread throughout the Los Angeles area that Jones had buried $30,000 of stolen loot near the Sierra Madre hide-out. That likely originated with Frank Lewis's claim that Jones had shown him "a suitcase full of gold," saying "there was thirty thousand 'Iron men.'"

For months, fortune hunters scoured the area, digging in the rocky soil in search of the treasure of Sierra Madre. They found nothing.

Officials, who had discovered all of twenty-six cents on Jones's dead body, made plans to bury him in a potter's field. None of his Jones-Lewis gang cohorts stepped forward to assist with burial costs. After all, they were either dead or in prison.

And Jones's father wasn't interested; he sent the following telegram from Missouri:

"Am the father of Dale Jones, killed by members of your office last Monday. Will have nothing to do with him or his burial. Disowned him years ago. Signed, Paul Jones"

But Margie's mother intervened.

Dale and Margie were buried side by side in a common grave in Los Angeles's Calvary Cemetery, a Catholic priest conducting a brief ceremony for a small group of mourners.

The headstone reads merely Marie "Margie" Celano.

| 8 |

'Agate Eyes'

"It is seldom that a woman, especially if she is very hand-some, is convicted in the courts of today. ... Mattie Howard is said to be a graduate of a convent and according to all reports is very handsome."
The Leavenworth Post, October 27, 1918

As Mattie Howard continued waiting for her murder trial and her former friends fell by the wayside, the local constabulary made her life miserable.

"I couldn't leave Jackson County, and there was not a cop or man on the police force who didn't take a great pleasure in running me in every time there was a crime committed in Kansas City," she said later. "I tried to work. I had several jobs and was fired from all of them when the police told my boss about me. ...

"I finally got so that when anything happened in the city, I would call the station and ask them if they wanted me to come in. I would save them the time of sending a man out for me."

Perhaps the police would not have been so obsessed with Mattie if she hadn't constantly hung around outlaws. Not only was her associ-ation with Dale Jones and his gang known, but she also continued to consort with Sam Taylor.

Even while Mattie was out on bond for the Morino murder in which Taylor was still considered a suspect, the two were arrested together twice — both times well beyond the confines of Jackson County.

First, police in Leavenworth, Kansas, recognized Mattie and Sam and nabbed them at a boarding house. Finding each with more than $200 in cash, they jailed the pair on an "investigation charge" before quickly releasing them.

A few months later, Mattie and Sam faced a much more serious situation.

This time they found their way to St. Louis, where Mattie's sister Marie lived with her husband, George Pappas. Within about a week of their arrival, police were knocking on the door of a second-floor room in a boarding house at 3547 Laclede Avenue that Mattie and Sam had rented under the names Mr. and Mrs. Rogers.

St. Louis police had received a tip suggesting they check out that address after an incident the previous night in which outlaws with a sawed-off shotgun fired at a police car pursuing them.

At 6 a.m. March 22, 1919, four officers charged into the Laclede Avenue room, where they found Mattie, Sam Taylor, and George and Marie Pappas — and much more.

The inventory included a sawed-off shotgun, a pint of nitroglycerin, two jimmies, saws, shotgun shells, fuses, two blackjacks, skeleton keys (used for working tumblers of safes), and other burglars' tools. The police also found a notebook listing about seventy-five businesses, many with the types of safes they had.

The officers arrested all four of the room's occupants and hauled them off to jail.

Taylor told police his name was Frances Sanders, then Jim Davis, George Davis, Sam Taylor, and William J. Hall. When he was tried five months later on a felony charge of having burglar tools, it was under the name George Davis.

Mattie said variously that she was Mrs. Davis, Mrs. Rogers, and Mrs. Sanders. At the police station, she admitted that she and Taylor (whom she called Jim Davis) weren't married but had met a year earlier in Oklahoma and had been traveling together. They had been involved in some trouble in Kansas City, she said.

"We were brought back there," she told St. Louis cop William A. Moller at the police station, "and Jim beat his case and put one over on the bulls in Kansas City."

Prosecutors in Kansas City had dropped the charges against Taylor in the Morino murder shortly after police escorted him and Mattie from Raton, New Mexico, but they eventually would refile them.

Mattie gave Moller a further assessment of her alleged accomplices.

"If Jim Davis would stay sober, he was one of the best pete men (safecrackers) in the country and a good money getter," she said, adding, "George Pappas was a good man, but green in the business."

Taylor wound up being the only of the four to be prosecuted. He sat in a St. Louis jail cell until August, when — with Jesse James Jr. defending him and with Mattie on hand for moral support — he was convicted on the burglary-tool charge and sentenced to five years in the state penitentiary.

Mattie was charged in the St. Louis case but freed on bond. She returned to Kansas City.

* * *

It seemed as if nobody wanted Mattie to actually stand trial for murder.

Already postponed from its original date in October 1918 to January 1919, her trial was delayed again to May 1919 when Assistant Prosecuting Attorney I.M. Lee asked for a continuance, claiming that one of the state's most important witnesses was ill.

In May, Judge Ralph S. Latshaw granted another continuance, this time to September 8 at the request of Jesse James Jr., who cited his own illness.

The delays gave us at *The Star* time to get creative. On June 6, 1919, we printed an in-depth story by fellow reporter Marcel Wallenstein that summarized and updated the Mattie Howard saga one year after the murder of Joe Morino.

It also included the first mention of her "agate eyes."

Under the headline "A Mystery of Agate Eyes," the story described the woman seen at the Touraine Apartment Hotel two days before the murder as a blond "whose most noticeable feature was her eyes, described as agate blue, with a cool, steady, fascinating fixity of expression that immediately focused the attention of anyone to whom she might be talking." Later, "The mysterious blond woman with the agate blue eyes had disappeared, leaving behind, apparently, no clew to her identity."

The "agate eyes" thing wasn't my idea, and in all the reporting on the case over the previous year by three Kansas City newspapers, there was no mention that the Touraine blond — or Mattie, for that matter — had distinct eyes. Now she was a "blond woman with ... calm agate blue eyes."

I have to admit that Mattie's eyes weren't all that remarkable, but the tried-and-true newspaper tradition of slapping a nickname on an emerging public figure worked. "The Girl with the Agate Eyes" stuck, no doubt helping elevate her in public awareness from a common criminal to a gangster of note.

The Star article of June 6, 1919, focused not only on Mattie but on the mysterious killing, describing it as "a murder staged with all the concomitants of a scenario plot and as pregnant with mystery and suggestive clews as a Katherine Green detective story."

It concluded: "... The Morino case is still shrouded in mystery, with its many 'clews' leading everywhere and nowhere, waiting an expert hand to weave its frazzled ends together."

* * *

With Taylor sitting in a St. Louis jail, Albert Pagel in the state penitentiary, and Dale Jones, Blackie Lancaster, and Frank Lewis dead, you'd think Mattie might have been running low on running mates. But not so.

A gangster and ex-con named Tony Cruye became her new pal.

Cruye had been in the Missouri penitentiary off and on since 1904. In 1916, he had been thrown in jail for attacking a police officer, chewing on the cop's hand in the process.

By 1919, he headed his own gang, and on July 20, 1919, he and Mattie were arrested together. The headline read "'Agate Eyes' held again," and my story opened: "Mattie Howard, 'the girl with the agate eyes,' and Tony Cruye, notoriously known to the police, were charged today with robbing the safe of Dr. J.H. Robinson Saturday night in the National Reserve Bank Building."

The job they were accused of pulling was "one of the most daring in local police annals," according to *The Journal*, and netted the perpetrators more than $5,000 in cash and jewelry.

Using a sledgehammer and a chisel during the overnight hours, the robbers cracked a safe in a third-floor office shared by a physician and a dentist. Horace Tucker, a night watchman in the building at 10th and Main, was on the second floor when he heard noises on the floor above. As he went to investigate, a man ran past him, knocking him to the floor.

Just before the incident, Tucker had seen a man and a woman in the hallway. He later identified Mattie as the woman but couldn't ID the man.

Also, Paul Weitkam, a police detective lurking across the street, said he saw Mattie and Cruye in the building's lobby at about the time of the robbery. He said they left the building and climbed into a waiting car with two men in it. Weitkam noted the license-plate number and later identified the car as Cruye's.

It was all circumstantial evidence but still damning.

Mattie, already out on bond in the Morino murder and the St. Louis burglary-tools cases, was arrested in her room at 915 Harrison Street. She and Cruye were charged with burglary and larceny and released on $3,000 bonds.

Two other men were arrested in the case a few days later: Charles "Spider" Kelly, who told police his name was Albert Taylor (in homage to Mattie's lovers/companions Albert Pagel and Sam Taylor perhaps?)

and Arthur "Fighting" Davis. Both were members of Cruye's gang. Cruye, Kelly, and Davis had been arrested together July 5 for car theft, but that case was dismissed when the complaining witnesses did not appear.

Similarly, the charges against Cruye, Kelly, Davis, and Mattie were dismissed at their preliminary hearing August 18 because of lack of evidence.

Within a week, Cruye and Kelly were back at it.

On August 25, they, along with two other men, put on masks, rushed into the Merchants' Hotel at Ninth and Broadway, kicked in the door of a fourth-floor room, and shouted, "Hands up!" Their goal was to hold up a high-stakes poker game. Instead, they were greeted by a volley of gunshots.

The four would-be robbers quickly retreated. Cruye, who was leading the charge, was hit in his right lung. He stumbled onto the elevator as the other three raced down the stairway.

Cruye was dead by the time the elevator reached the first floor.

Kelly and the other two, Tom Hand and Charles Bell, were quickly arrested, with a police officer shooting Bell in the right thigh in the process. They pleaded not guilty to attempted first-degree robbery.

* * *

With Tony Cruye joining the ever-growing list of Mattie's unfortunate accomplices, perhaps Kansas City's underworld finally was wising up to the fact that the men who associated with her were more likely to wind up dead than wealthy.

In any case, after the charges against her in the heist at the National Reserve Bank Building were dropped and Cruye was killed, she managed to keep her name out of the newspapers for a few months. That would change in a big way with her murder trial, delayed again from September until October.

But first came the return of Albert Pagel, the man for whom Mattie had abandoned her husband and launched a life of crime.

After Pagel entered the Missouri penitentiary in August 1918 on a grand larceny conviction, Mattie had said, "I never loved but one man and that was Albert Pagel," and, "My heart is in a cell in Jefferson City. When Albert is free, I will reform and be happy."

Well, on October 10, 1919, with the start of his sweetheart's trial only days away, Pagel walked out of the state pen after serving less than fourteen months of a two-and-half-year term.

The Pathway of Mattie Howard indicates Pagel went immediately to Kansas City for a reunion with Mattie and "brought a ray of gladness into her despondent heart." He also took a meeting with attorney Jesse James Jr. in which he "threatened to blow the latter's brains out if he did not try to free Mattie from the murder charge and save her from prison."

Obviously, reform was not on Albert's mind.

Ten days after Pagel got out of prison, a crew decided to blow the safe at a downtown cigar store that had been known to house one of the city's largest gambling operations. Unfortunately, the would-be burglars hadn't done their homework. A police anti-vice campaign had shut down the gambling den a few days earlier, and the safe held only fifteen dollars.

Worse, employees at the neighboring Hotel Dixon heard the commotion in the cigar store and notified the police, who descended on the building before the bad guys could get away. A shootout ensued outside the business between three police officers and four bandits.

A bullet hit twenty-three-year-old patrolman Frederick F. Tierney in the chest, and when he fell to the sidewalk, a gunman put two more bullets into him. Tierney died later that day at General Hospital.

One of the men attempting to escape, Clyde Esterbrook, was wounded and captured. The other three escaped.

Within days, Roy Gossett and Edward Higgins were arrested in connection with the burglary attempt. Robert E. Phelan, Kansas City's chief of detectives, insisted that the final member of the crew was none other than the recently released Albert Pagel.

Moreover, Esterbrook claimed that he hadn't shot Tierney to death, Pagel had, and a taxi driver reportedly identified Pagel as the shooter. The police never picked up Pagel, and Esterbrook eventually pleaded guilty to the killing and received a life sentence.

* * *

After the botched burglary and fatal shooting, Pagel apparently had the good sense to stay out of the public eye for a few months. He was nowhere to be found during Mattie's murder trial.

Pagel's presence likely would have reflected poorly on Mattie, and, with Jesse James Jr. as her lawyer, she would need all the help she could get — even though the prosecution had a totally circumstantial case.

Witnesses would identify her as the woman who accompanied Joe Morino to the Touraine two days before the murder, but nobody could put her in the room where the murder occurred or even in the hotel at the time of the murder.

The prosecution also had a bad check for a hundred dollars with Mattie's signature and the claims of Morino's chief clerk that his boss had a relationship with her, but that hardly added up to murder.

With no eyewitnesses to the killing, no murder weapon, and not even a definite time of death, an acquittal seemed entirely possible. Add in the fact that women accused of murder — especially attractive women — were rarely convicted by the all-male juries of that era, and Mattie likely was feeling good about her chances.

Unfortunately for her, Jackson County juries weren't always averse to convicting women of murder.

Although nineteen-year-old Rose Peterson was found innocent of second-degree murder in 1909 after shooting her husband three times, claiming he had slapped her, others among K.C.'s female killers weren't so lucky.

Lula Prince Kennedy was sentenced to ten years and Aggie Myers to hang (later commuted to life in prison) for killing their husbands in 1901 and 1904, respectively.

Clara T. Schweiger got fifteen years for shooting her ex-husband to death in a Kansas City courthouse after the ruling in a custody hearing went against her in 1915.

Even Sophia Bell, a sympathetic defendant if there ever was one, was convicted.

In 1911, Bell had given refuge to a seventeen-year-old girl named Nydia Bernard from her abusive husband. When that husband tried to force his way into Bell's house to get at his young bride, Bell gunned him down. She was sentenced to two years for manslaughter in 1913 after originally being charged with second-degree murder.

The judge for the trials of Peterson, Schweiger, and Bell was Ralph S. Latshaw — who also would be on the bench for Mattie Howard's trial.

Born in Canada in 1865, Latshaw lived virtually his entire life in Kansas City, attending public schools before heading off to Georgetown University in Washington, D.C. He was elected as criminal court judge in 1908 at the age of forty-three.

The Star said of Latshaw, a staunch Democrat and a Boss Tom Pendergast supporter, in a 1932 obituary: "Quick-tempered and outspoken, he was impatient of opposition that seemed trivial and of legal practices that did not seem to him obviously candid and sincere. ... Judge Latshaw was regarded as one of the most severe judges who ever sat upon the criminal bench and that he often 'went the limit' in his sentences against confirmed lawbreakers."

In 1910, he presided over what remains the most famous murder trial in Kansas City history, when Dr. Bennett Clarke Hyde was accused of poisoning real estate developer and philanthropist Col. Thomas H. Swope, who died, and other members of the Swope family. Hyde, who was married to Swope's niece, was convicted after a monthlong trial, but the Missouri Supreme Court overturned the verdict. Despite three attempts at retrial, no verdict was ever sustained against Hyde.

Latshaw also developed a close relationship with Jesse James Jr., who at one time worked for his law firm, Latshaw & Latshaw. *The Star* noted in a 1915 story about the funeral of notorious outlaw Frank

James that his nephew, Jesse James Jr., and Judge Ralph Latshaw were among the mourners.

Less than five years later, Latshaw would preside over the biggest trial of Jesse James Jr.'s legal career — with Mattie's fate on the line. The relationship between the judge and the bandit's son couldn't hurt Mattie's cause.

On the other hand, Jesse James Jr.'s record in criminal cases — and murder cases in particular — hardly inspired confidence.

| 9 |

Murder Trial

"Mattie Howard's trial was one of the most spectacular in Kansas City's court history. She was a crime leader — a cold planner of crimes, so asserted the detectives who coped with her keen mind."
The Kansas City Times, May 17, 1928

Mattie Howard's second-degree murder trial began on October 20, 1919, in the Jackson County Courthouse. The building, which featured Romanesque revival architecture, was at Fifth and Oak streets, just east of the then-sixty-two-year-old business and entertainment area known as the City Market. It had been the venue for all of Kansas City's major criminal trials since opening in 1892.

This one became one of the most notorious.

Over six days, local newspapers covered the proceedings in great detail, especially when it came to the appearance and demeanor of the woman on trial. Here is a condensed and combined version of my reportage (with additional color from *The Post* and *The Journal*).

Jackson County Courthouse
Missouri Valley Special Collections, Kansas City Public Library, Kansas City, Missouri

Day One

Mattie Howard to Trial

The trial of Mattie Howard on a second-degree murder charge in connection with the killing of Joseph Morino, "diamond king," began Tuesday morning in Judge Ralph S. Latshaw's division of the criminal court. Proof that Howard was in Kansas City in May 1918 when Morino was slain in the Touraine apartments, Fourteenth and Central streets, will be produced by the prosecution, Edward J. Curtin, assistant prosecutor, said in opening the case. Howard always has contended she was in Oklahoma at the time of the murder.

Howard was accompanied in court only by her attorney, Jesse James. She appeared calm and was dressed stylishly in a brown coat with fur collar and cuffs.

Beauty and Mystery Blend as Attractions in Mattie Howard Trial

"Why, she couldn't commit murder! She's too pretty."

True, it was an impressionable youth in a snug, green, belted suit who was speaking. But an old man in baggy trousers shifted his tobacco quid and nodded approval to the sentiments. Many of the men who have seen Mattie Howard in Judge Ralph S. Latshaw's courtroom feel that way about it.

Whether the jury does is another matter. Its members, principally, are middle aged, sensible looking men who probably wear rubbers and carry home the family beefsteak on the streetcar. But sometimes they…

Well, anyway, the woman who is facing that jury in Judge Latshaw's court with a possibility of prison bars looming before her doesn't seem to be worrying any. If she knows who murdered Joseph Morino, "diamond king," at the Touraine apartments in May 1918, she isn't telling anything about it by her face. She sits immobile all day long, never so much as fluttering one of her long, dark curling eyelashes over her opalescent eyes.

It is an unwritten law that a jury never convicts a pretty woman. Howard has more than beauty. She has mystery. And when blond women are mysterious, they are more baffling than the most subtle brunettes.

Although Howard sits calm and unperturbed, her face is not hard. The prosecution will insist she is cold and heartless. But from a side view, her profile is almost gentle. Her face, with its slightly Grecian nose and its frame of golden hair, is such as is seen sometimes in portraits of saints. When she turns her full face, she becomes baffling. In contrast with the reserve of her profile, her lips are unusually full and seem to express the passion the rest of her face lacks.

Her eyes seem to be continually changing, both in color and expression.

None of the spectators in the courtroom would pick the inconspicuous, quietly dressed woman sitting at the attorney's table for a "queen of the bandits," for a "nemesis of men," or any of the other characters she has been represented as portraying. In the words of the men in the courtroom, "she'd pass anywhere."

"I'd pick her for a saleswoman in a woman's clothing store," said one.

Howard appears modishly and sensibly dressed. She wears a brown suede cloak with fur collar and cuffs, a blue serge dress very simply made, and a turban of gray and black velvet. Brown calfskin shoes of the "sensible" type with Cuban heels cover her small, well-shaped feet. A strand of gold beads about her throat and earrings, made of $2.50 gold pieces, match her golden hair. She wears a single ring with a sapphire setting on the small finger of her right hand. Her skin is ivory in tone, and she wears no "makeup."

The woman who is alleged to have upset the hearts of men, both of the under and upper world, makes no conscious effort to charm in the courtroom. She sits by the side of her attorney, Jesse James, listening intently to every word of testimony, yawning quite often during the arguments of attorneys but seldom bestowing a glance upon the jury. Her hands lie calmly clasped in her lap. The references of Edward J. Curtin, assistant prosecutor, and James P. Aylward, a special prosecutor hired by the Morino estate, to "Morino's body" and to the details of the murder do not cause her even to suppress a yawn.

She seems to have no woman friends, or at least they do not appear in court with her. At times she is the only woman in the courtroom.

She is cold and heartless, say some. Detective Harry Arthur, who trailed her to New Mexico and arrested her two weeks after the murder of Morino, says she is devoid of emotion. Others say she is sinned against, a "goat" of the workings of justice. Still others credit her with the brains and the indomitable will that has directed bandit gangs.

Which of these she is, a jury of men will decide.

Day Two

'Woman Paid the Rent'

Mattie Howard, "the girl with the agate eyes," was positively identified late yesterday afternoon as the woman who rented an apartment at the Touraine Apartment Hotel, 1412 Central Street, with Joe Morino, murdered diamond king. Walter Geraughty, clerk at the hotel, told a jury in Judge Ralph S. Latshaw's division of criminal court that Miss Howard and Morino visited the apartment house about noon May 23, 1918.

"The woman inquired for an apartment," Geraughty said. "I took them to apartment No. 301, and Miss Howard said it was a nice place and they would take it. She gave me twenty dollars for a week's rent in advance. That is the woman sitting right there beside the table," he remarked, pointing to Miss Howard.

The accused woman looked him straight in the eye when he made the statement. Unlike many another woman who has been tried in the criminal court on a murder charge, she showed no signs of emotion. Not once did she sob, and not a tear dampened her eyelashes during the entire day while she listened stoically to the testimony of the state's witnesses.

Geraughty said he became suspicious of the occupants of the apartment because it was so quiet. He said there was never a call for ice water, clean linen, or for a porter or a bell boy.

"They didn't even ask to have the garbage removed," he said.

The body was discovered two days later, he said, by a porter, who was attracted to the apartment by the odor.

The state endeavored to show that Morino left his store on Thursday night to meet the Howard woman at the apartment hotel by the testimony of T.K. Elliott, a bookkeeper in a bank. Elliott kept Morino's books for him at night and always helped with the inventory. He detailed a telephone conversation Morino held with a woman unknown to Elliott. The conversation, as he heard Morino speak, follows:

"Hello, this is Morino. Been waiting to hear from you about that. Everything's all right. Touraine Hotel. In the house or in the street? That's near Fourteenth and Central. About 9:20. All right."

Morino then turned to him and remarked, Elliott testified:

"Where's that Howard woman's check?"

Morino was referring to a bad check for a hundred dollars from a "Miss M. Howard," Elliott said, and he looked for it in the files.

"I was unable to find it, and Morino told me to let it go, that he probably would get along all right without it," Elliott said.

The theory advanced by the state is that Morino answered the call, to be beaten to death by a heavy "blackjack." Elliott also said Morino wore two diamonds when he left the store.

Zefferino Gamba, a clerk in the Morino store, said he had seen Mattie three or four times in the store and identified her as the woman who bought the diamond bar pin for $140.

On the night of May 23, Gamba testified, Morino was called to the telephone, and subsequent to a conversation over the wire turned and asked for "that Howard woman's check." Later, when Gamba and Mattie met in the office of the chief of police, Gamba testified she recognized him.

J.F. Wiley, an embalmer who handled the body, testified as to the time necessary before decomposition set in, an important link to the state's chain of circumstantial evidence, for the body was in extremely bad condition when discovered the following Saturday, according to the embalmer and Dr. J.S. Snider, deputy coroner. The state is attempting to prove Mattie Howard was in the city on Thursday night and that Morino met his death at that time.

Day Three

State Scores Again in the Howard Trial

C.V. Floyd of Miami, Florida, identified Mattie Howard as the woman he saw in the Nance café on the night of May 23. Floyd, who said he was registered at the Hotel Baltimore then, testified that a blond woman, with peculiar blue eyes, sat at a table near him, and that just prior to leaving she wrote a note on a small pocket pad, which she left with a check girl, who took it to the table. Floyd swore that the note contained these words:

"You will greatly please me by calling Home Main 3085 or Bell 1780, Apartment 301."

He said that he called the numbers later in the night but received no answer. He testified that on the following day he read of the murder and looked up the telephone numbers. They were at the Touraine apartments, he said.

Another important witness in counteracting the defense's expected attempt at an alibi was Richard Hauer, 504 Woodland Avenue, who was a taxi driver at the time of the murder. He identified Mattie Howard and Sam Taylor as the couple he drove from the Touraine apartments to the Fredric Hotel, near Ninth and Oak streets, early on the morning of Friday, May 24, 1918. He said that he had received the call at 12:55 o'clock on that morning.

Daniel H. Cox of the Midwest National Bank testified that Mattie Howard opened an account there on February 14, 1918, and that he was familiar with her handwriting. He identified her writing on the register at the Touraine apartments as "B. Stanley and wife." He also identified her signature on hotel registers as "Anna B. Brooks" at Dawson, New Mexico; "Dorothy Emerson" at Dallas, Texas; "Mrs. F.B. Vanders" at Trinidad, Colorado; and "Mrs. Moore" at Tulsa, Oklahoma.

During the trial yesterday, Judge Ralph S. Latshaw of the criminal court received a large box of American beauty roses addressed to Mattie Howard in his care. He gave it to a deputy marshal with instructions to deliver it to Jesse James, her attorney, in the Scarritt Building. It was from some person whose name was not signed to the card. The following message was in large handwriting on the card:

"Hoping this will bring a little ray of cheer and comfort into these hours of darkness. From the woman friend who asked you to call her up each night to let her know that you are safe, and who wishes to help you in any way possible if you will let her know the need."

At the recess, Miss Howard received her roses and brought one of them into court with her. Most of the time after that she sat behind her attorney, the rose pressed to her nostrils, the note on the table beside her, listening to the testimony, and occasionally smiling a bit.

Regardless of how damaging the evidence of the state may be, nothing seems to shock her calm demeanor. Not once in the trial has she exhibited any emotion, other than a slight smile now and then. She pays close attention to the testimony, watching its effect on the jury.

Day Four

State Builds Circumstantial Case About Mattie Howard

Can a web of circumstantial evidence separate Mattie Howard from her phenomenal luck — or is it luck? Will the wealth of incriminating testimony introduced by the state in her trial for the murder of Joe Morino, diamond broker, send the woman of devious paths to the penitentiary?

The state rested its case late Thursday after more than a score of witnesses had testified. The defense began introducing testimony immediately.

The courtroom was crowded at the afternoon session, and many persons tried in vain to hear evidence.

Howard again was identified as the woman who registered at the Touraine apartments with the "diamond king" during the morning session in Judge Ralph S. Latshaw's court. Ira Allen, Negro porter at the apartments, said he saw Howard come to the Touraine with Morino and that they registered as "Mr. and Mrs. B. Stanley, Detroit." Allen said he saw Howard pay twenty dollars for the apartment and that he carried her grip to her room.

Allen also told of finding Morino's body in the hall of the apartment Saturday, May 25, three days after the couple had registered there.

Allen said he went to Apartment 301 every day to get garbage, after Howard and Morino moved in, but there was no evidence that the kitchenette had been used. He did not notice an odor, he said, until Saturday. That caused him to investigate, and he found the pawnbroker's body lying in the hallway.

A bathmat was under the dead man's head, there was shot from a blackjack on the floor, and the blinds in the living room were drawn, Allen said.

Howard listened intently to the porter's description of Morino's body but showed no emotion.

"Was there any way in which a person could get out of Apartment 301 other than by going through the hotel lobby?" Allen was asked.

"Yes, there was a back exit through the basement that could be used," he said.

The testimony of Mrs. Joseph Morino, widow of the murdered man, was read late Thursday, and contradicted, according to Jesse James, attorney for Miss Howard, the testimony given by Allen that Morino must have stayed away from home on the night of May 23. Mrs. Morino accounted fully for Morino's whereabouts on May 23, the defense maintains, when she declared she had supper with him that day, that he stayed at home that night, and that she was with him at other times during the day of May 23.

A.C. Gresham of St. Paul, Arkansas, and his wife identified Taylor from a picture produced in court as the man who registered May 18, 1918, with Mattie Howard at the Southern rooming house in Joplin, Missouri, as Mr. and Mrs. Robinson. Gresham, at the time the proprietor of the rooming house, testified Taylor and Mattie left their rooms May 21, returning May 26. They left again the night of May 26, according to the witness, in a motor car.

Through it all, Mattie Howard, the inscrutable, sits composed and quiet. Her strikingly cold blue eyes gaze out over the courtroom without revealing a vestige of emotion. Once, it is said, she loved diamonds, but she wears none at her trial. Instead are ornaments of heavy gold design. Gold $2.50 coins are pendant from her ears, a chain of fat gold beads encircles her neck, a gold watch is strapped to one wrist, and a gold signet ring gleams dully on one finger.

Such is Mattie Howard, the woman in the case in so many affairs of the underworld, that domain without borders.

Mattie Howard to Testify

Jesse James, attorney for Mattie Howard, arose when the state rested its case and filed a general demurrer, asking the case be dismissed. Judge Ralph S. Latshaw overruled the demurrer, whereupon James said Mattie would take the stand in her own defense.

"How do you feel now," Miss Howard was asked after the state had finished its case.

"Just as good as I did before it started," she laughed, munching peanut brittle from a paper bag on the table. "It's all very interesting to me."

Miss Howard wasn't at all backward in talking about herself, unless the questions happened to touch on the case. Questions of that nature she referred to her attorney.

"Yes, I was reared in Denver," she said, "and educated in a convent. I attended St. Mary's Academy from the time I was nine years old until I was seventeen."

Miss Howard is now twenty-four years old.

"How did you happen to break over from a life of a convent bred girl to lead a life of the road," she was asked.

"Now, I'll have to refer you to my attorney," she laughed. "Possibly after this case is over I can tell you all about it, but not now."

When the afternoon session adjourned, Miss Howard stood on the landing in the criminal court building, facing the county jail, waiting for her attorney. From the point where she stood she could see men prisoners confined in their cells across the area way. She laughed and joked with them, telling them how her trial was progressing.

Mattie Howard May Enter 'Movies' if Freed of Murder

If Mattie Howard is acquitted of the second-degree murder charge in connection with the killing of Joseph Morino, wealthy "diamond broker" found dead in the Touraine apartments, Fourteenth and Central streets in May 1918, she may go into the movies. That became known Friday.

Miss Howard seemed more confident than ever that she would be acquitted. She is a good vocalist and a remarkable pianist. Of course, musical talent will not secure her a berth in the "movie" world, but there are other attributes possessed by the defendant in the Morino case whose future rests in the hands of twelve jurymen now hearing the trial in Judge Ralph S. Latshaw's division of the criminal court.

It may be the penitentiary — but Mattie Howard seems to have eliminated conviction entirely from jury decisions. It is understood an offer to enter the "screen game" has been made to the defendant.

Mattie Howard, now twenty-four years old, was graduated from a Denver, Colorado, academy just seven years ago, and has spent much of her time working as a telephone operator. Her mother is living at Raton, New Mexico, with a younger brother and sister.

According to friends, when Miss Howard lived in Colorado she was known as one of the best girl athletes in the academy. She loved horses and mountain hikes. She now is of the "perfect thirty-six" type and a striking blond.

Day Five

Fight to Prove an Alibi

Mattie Howard's alibi that she was in Oklahoma at the time of the murder was strengthened by witnesses for the defense Friday morning. Angelo Bersi, who conducts a furniture store in Picher, Oklahoma, testified he saw Howard in that city on May 24 and 25. She was with Sam Taylor, he said. Bersi said he knew Howard by sight, having seen her in Picher previously.

He particularly remembers her being there at that time, he said, because a Red Cross drive was on, and all persons passing by Red Cross headquarters were "arrested" and fined small contributions for the cause. Howard, he said, was brought in with a group of women.

Lon Freeman, policeman, of Picher, testified he saw Howard in that town at 3 o'clock in the morning of May 25. He was in a restaurant across the street from the Angelus Hotel, he said. Howard stopped at the restaurant, Freeman said, and he carried her grip to the hotel for her. He said he knew Howard as Mrs. George Moore.

James E. Spencer, another policeman of Picher, testified he saw Howard in Picher on that date.

Depositions corroborating this testimony were read from Walter Satterlee, Albert Bryant, and Mrs. Maude Bryant. Mrs. Bryant testified Howard ate supper at the Bryant boarding house on May 25.

The deposition of Ethera Pounter, proprietor of the Angelus Hotel at Picher, identified her as the woman who spent the night of May 24 at the hotel.

'Agate Eyes' on the Stand

Mattie Howard looked straight at the twelve men who are to determine her innocence or guilt, late yesterday afternoon, and denied that she murdered Joseph Morino in an apartment at the Touraine apartments in May 1918. Miss Howard is on trial for Morino's murder in Judge Ralph S. Latshaw's division of the criminal court.

The courtroom was filled to capacity all day long. All the standing room was taken, and when Miss Howard took the stand, the doors had to be closed to prevent those unable to get in from pushing those in front too close to the counsel table and jury box. Friends of Miss Howard sat beside her during the afternoon before she took the stand, the first time any of them have appeared open in court. Everyone was anxious to see the woman of the "agate eyes," and when she took the stand there was much craning of necks and stretching of toes on the part of spectators.

The woman denied she had an apartment at the Touraine, where Morino's body was found, denied that she went there with Morino, denied that she registered there, denied that she was in Kansas City on either of the days this murder may have been committed.

After asking her several questions tending to establish her identity, Jesse James, her attorney, asked her point blank if she murdered Morino. Looking directly at the jury she answered:

"No, I did not murder Joe Morino."

The young woman, who spent her childhood in a convent and who is now known as the "Queen of the Bandits" and "the girl with the agate eyes," was as calm and stoical when she took the stand as she has been throughout the trial. She spoke in a low, well-modulated voice, clearly and distinctly, so that each word could be heard by all the jurymen. Even when she became confused upon cross-examination and became mixed in her dates, she retained her calmness.

In cross-examination, Mattie Howard frequently used the answer "I don't remember." She stared at the jurors intently while she spoke.

Once, when Edward J. Curtin and James P. Aylward attempted to connect her name with Dale Jones, "Blackie" Lancaster, Tony Cruye, and several other criminals, all of whom have been killed or sent to the penitentiary, she became angry. The attorneys for the state shot the questions at her so fast and she answered so hurriedly in such a loud voice that the objections of her attorney and the rulings of Judge Latshaw on the objections were lost.

"Were you ever associated with Dale Jones?"

"Didn't he give you that string of gold beads you now have around your neck?"

"Weren't you associated with 'Blackie' Lancaster?"

"Weren't you arrested at Tenth and Main streets with Tony Cruye?"

"Weren't you known as Mrs. George Moore, and isn't George Moore serving a term in the penitentiary?"

"Didn't your brother (Oliver), Sam Taylor, and George Moore serve a term in the Leavenworth penitentiary for robbing a post office at Trinidad, Colorado?"

Those were some of the questions shot at Miss Howard by the attorneys for the state. In answer to each she said no, her voice growing louder with each answer so that the jury could hear. Her attorney had jumped to his feet with the first question and objected, the court sustaining the objection. But the questions and answers came so fast that the interference of her attorney was useless.

The Dale Jones and "Blackie" Lancaster referred to were leaders of the most dangerous band of outlaws that have operated in this section of the country in recent years. A statement by Miss Howard brought up that line of questioning. She said she lived in a downtown hotel but moved because she "didn't like the class of people who frequented the place." The attorneys for the prosecution then asked question after question regarding some of the men with whom the state claims she associated.

Miss Howard became confused slightly in her dates upon cross-examination. She said she was in Tulsa, Oklahoma, May 22 and 23, and in Picher, Oklahoma, May 24. The state contends Morino was killed the night of May 23.

Depositions of the defense read in court tended to show Miss Howard was in Picher the afternoon of May 24, remaining there for dinner and overnight. On direct examination, Miss Howard testified she arrived in Picher the afternoon of Friday, May 24, coming from Tulsa. On cross-examination, she was unable to say just when she left Tulsa but that she thought it was in the afternoon, arriving at Miami, Oklahoma, in the evening and then driving to Picher. Answering further questions, she denied that she went from Tulsa to Picher at all. Finally, a little later, she said she left Tulsa early in the morning, going by train to Miami and driving to Picher.

Miss Howard admitted upon cross-examination that she was with Sam Taylor in Picher on May 24, again in Joplin, Missouri, on May 26, that she saw him in Trinidad, Colorado, two months later, and that she was arrested in the same house with him at Raton, New Mexico, and again in St. Louis.

In an attempt to show that Morino was alive Friday night, May 24, and that the murder must have been committed that night, the defense placed Orla Puckett, night clerk at the Touraine, on the stand. He said that at about 8 o'clock that night a man and two women, one a blond and one a brunette, entered the apartment house and went upstairs. He did not know who the man was, he said, but his general description was that of Morino. He also said he did not believe either of the women was Miss Howard.

Orville Bailey, a milkman, testified that he saw two women hurriedly leaving the place about 4 o'clock Saturday morning while he was delivering milk to the apartments. One was hatless and the other wore her hat. He said he did not believe either of the women was Miss Howard.

Miss Howard was on the stand for two hours during the afternoon and will return for further cross-examination when court convenes this morning.

Day Six

Says Letters are Alike

Mattie Howard's handwriting, the state contends, resembles the signatures in the register of the Touraine Apartment Hotel where Joe Morino, Italian diamond broker, was lured to his death, and resembles the writing in the register of a Trinidad, Colorado, hotel where she was the night before her arrest. It is similar also to writing of a note said to have been sent by her to C.V. Floyd of Miami, Florida, in a Kansas City café, the state contends further.

On cross-examination Saturday, the woman at first refused to attempt to imitate the signatures. Repeated attempts of the state to befuddle Miss Howard in cross-examination on the handwriting revealed that the young woman's denial of that part of testimony was based on evidence.

The writing was in backhand. Miss Howard asserted that she never wrote backhand but was taught Spencerian and wrote Spencerian on checks and all private papers.

The handwriting from the Touraine reads "B. Stanley and wife, Detroit." Miss Howard declared positively she did not write it.

"I don't write backhand," she declared repeatedly, when pressed by the state to copy the names.

Edward J. Curtin, assistant prosecutor, asked her to copy it off backhand as well as she could. In spite of the objections of her lawyer, she finally took a pencil and copied the names.

She made a copy, backhand, which resembled the hotel register writing but very little. It was passed to the jury, with other samples of her handwriting.

Mattie Howard was shown in the light of a companion of criminals and a burglar's accomplice for the first time since she has been on trial. It was not until the rebuttal that the state was given opportunity to assail her character. Friday on the witness stand, the defendant declared she moved from a Kansas City hotel because she did not like to associate with the sort of persons who frequented the place.

Because of that statement, the prosecution was permitted to recall William Moller, St. Louis police detective, who testified finding Mattie, Sam Taylor, and George Pappas and his wife together in a room in St. Louis last March. In the room, Moller testified, was a complete set of burglar tools, a sawed-off shotgun, a vial of nitroglycerin, percussion caps, fuse, and other materials used by safecrackers.

"She told me Taylor, alias Davis, was one of the best 'pete men' (safeblowers) in the country and a good money getter," Moller testified. "Pappas, she said, was a good man, but green in the business."

In the cross-examination that followed, the defendant emphatically denied she told Moller that "Sam Taylor was one of the best safe blowers in the country when he was sober."

The strain of the trial is beginning to tell on Mattie Howard. Her remarkable composure has begun to weaken. She seemed paler than usual and looked tired. With her customary lack of emotion, however, she denied the ordeal affected her.

Halt a Trial for Valera

Mattie Howard met Eamon de Valera, the so-called "President of the Irish Republic," late Saturday. The scene of the meeting was the crowded courtroom of Judge Ralph S. Latshaw, where she is on trial for alleged participation in the murder of Joe Morino, rich Kansas City pawnbroker, slain in the Touraine Apartment Hotel, 1412 Central Street, late in May 1918.

De Valera, a hero of the 1916 Easter Rebellion in the fight against British rule in Ireland, is touring America to raise funds and support for the Sinn Fein political party. Accompanied by two friends, he entered the courtroom shortly after 2:30 o'clock. Judge Latshaw smiled a greeting, as the distinguished visitor elbowed his way through the crowded aisle. Judge Latshaw signaled to the court bailiff to lead the jurors into an adjoining room and keep them there.

The judge stepped from behind his desk, shook de Valera's hand, then led him to the platform near the witness chair. Those in the courtroom, learning the identity of de Valera, began to cheer. The "Irish President" raised his hand for silence and began to speak. He talked of Ireland, then commented on the justice of American court procedure, which permits an accused person to get a fair and impartial trial before a jury of twelve men.

"In Ireland," de Valera added, "court trials are more or less a burlesque. They put you in jail and then forget all about you."

At the conclusion of his address, the courtroom crowd surged forward. De Valera shook hands with dozens of men and women. One of the first to reach him was Mattie Howard.

She turned her "agate eyes" on de Valera and seized his hand in a firm grip.

"Glad to meet you, Mr. President," she breathed, her cheeks glowing. "You're the first president I ever met. So glad you came."

De Valera smiled, then slowly withdrew his hand, extending it to James P. Aylward, a special prosecutor in the trial. De Valera later left the courtroom amid thunderous applause, and the jury was recalled to the box and the trial resumed.

Mattie Howard Shows Signs of Nervousness as She Completes Defense

When Mattie Howard stepped down from the witness stand in Judge Ralph S. Latshaw's criminal court Saturday after a driving cross-examination on details of the death of Joseph Morino, there were drawn lines about her eyes, and her hair, previously neat and well arranged, gave evidence of the disquiet which she seemed to be feeling.

Both the state and the defense rested their cases, and it was believed the fate of Miss Howard would go into the hands of the jury late Saturday.

One of the strongest cases of circumstantial evidence ever offered in Jackson County was made against Miss Howard by Edward J. Curtin, assistant prosecutor, and James P. Aylward, special prosecutor.

Aylward began the closing arguments to the jury at 2:50 o'clock Saturday afternoon, and after picturing the gruesome murder of Morino and reviewing the evidence as presented by the state, he scored the apparent cold-blooded attitude of Mattie Howard during the trial. He referred to her cold agate eyes and her alluring smile, and in a forceful plea for her conviction, asked the jurors not to sympathize with her because she was a woman, declaring that she was a "dangerous woman and not deserving of sympathy."

In his argument, Jesse James, attorney for the defense, said, "I am going to disappoint the state. I am not going to appeal to you for sympathy — all I want is justice, just justice."

James then began an attack on the testimony submitted by the state, which was to show that Morino went to the Touraine on Wednesday, May 22, 1918, and registered with Mattie Howard. He pointed out the fact that Mrs. Morino had testified that her husband was at home with her on that night and had attended a show with her.

James then attacked the testimony of C.V. Floyd, the Miami, Florida, man who said the defendant had flirted with him in Nance's café. James repeatedly referred to Floyd as a "volunteer witness," declaring that if he had acted in good faith, he would have given the information to the police before the month of June, following the murder.

He pointed out that Mrs. Corine Fleming, housekeeper at the Touraine, had testified that she and a five-year-old child were in Apartment 301 on Thursday, May 23, and that nobody was then in the room.

In concluding the state's argument, Curtin asked if the jurors were going to let Miss Howard smile her way through the trial, "as she probably had smilingly lured Morino to his death." He asked the jury to aid in wiping out the stain of crime in Kansas City by bringing in a verdict finding the defendant guilty of murder in the second degree.

Curtin also made a passionate plea for justice, picturing to the jury a dying man, and in guttural tones demonstrated how Morino must have died in agony.

In his closing speech to the jury, Curtin said she had "a heart as cold as the stone that rests on Joe Morino's grave."

Prisoner Shows No Emotion

The Mattie Howard trial was one of the most spectacular and complex murder cases tried in Kansas City for years, because of the unusual circumstances surrounding the killing of Joseph Morino, and also because of the mystery in which the defendant seemed to have been enshrouded.

"Underworld" habitues are said to have called her queen, and men of finance and prominence are said to have bowed to her hypnotic beauty. Her life was one of extremes, ranging from a chaste little convent girl of seven years ago to the "woman of the world" at the time of her trial.

Never before has the Jackson County Criminal Court held such a woman as the "Golden Girl." Not in the memory of the oldest employee has a woman ever been tried for murder in this county who at no stage of the trial exhibited emotion of any description.

Mattie Howard came into court last Monday morning smiling. Just before the jury came in for the start of the trial, she remarked with a smile in answer to a question:

"The verdict will be 'not guilty,' of course. What else could you expect?"

Miss Howard's attitude throughout the trial remained unchanged. Even while the jury was deliberating, she sent for grapes and chocolates, which she ate as she chatted with her attorney, Jesse James, and friends.

According to court attaches, more interest was shown in this case than in any other since the Hyde trial, and all during the hearing the court room was packed. Miss Howard, admittedly charming, had announced her intention of entering the "movies" if she were acquitted, and hundreds of women attended the trial to get a glimpse of the "convent girl," who was charged with so gruesome a crime as the murder of Joseph Morino.

To Agate Eyes, 12 years

Mattie Howard paused with a half-eaten grape between her fingers, swung her chair about so as to face the jury, and stopped eating from the paper sack in her lap while the jury that heard her case passed its verdict to Judge Ralph S. Latshaw in the criminal court Saturday night.

"We, the jury, find Mattie Howard guilty of second-degree murder for the death of Joseph Morino and assess her punishment at twelve years in the penitentiary," read Judge Latshaw.

"Is that your verdict, gentlemen?" asked the judge.

"It is," the jurors replied.

Mattie's dark, seeping eyelashes, more noticeable because of their direct contrast with her blond hair, dropped over her agate blue eyes, but only for a moment. A slight flush of color that tinged her face passed swiftly as she regained control of herself. The half-eaten grape was raised to her lips, and vanished. The empty hand slipped back to her lap, to rest idly beside the one that clasped the paper sack filled with grapes, which took the place of dinner.

It was then 8:35 o'clock. The jury had deliberated an hour and forty minutes.

Jesse James, the woman's attorney, called for a poll of the jury. Judge Latshaw called for the list of jurors and instructed them to say in answer to their names, "This is my verdict," or "This is not my verdict." As the first name was called, Miss Howard looked at the judge, and as the answer came, she looked at the juror. At the answer that "this is my verdict," not even her eyelashes moved.

Seven ballots had been taken by the jurors. The first was for "guilty." The next ballot was on the period of confinement. It stood one for five years, one for ninety-five, five for ten, and five for twenty. Five more ballots were required before twelve years was agreed upon. Under the law, the minimum sentence is ten years and the maximum life in the penitentiary.

A majority of the crowd that remained all evening without dinner, awaiting the verdict, was disappointed. The consensus of opinion was that she would be discharged, chiefly because she was a woman, and then again the sympathy of many of those in the courtroom was with the "Golden Girl."

There hasn't been such a large gathering of Kansas City's underworld in one place at one time as there has been at Mattie Howard's trial. At one time or another her name has been linked with the names of many men notorious for their deeds outside the pale of the law: Dale Jones, "Blackie" Lancaster, Tony Cruye, all of whom have died with "their boots on" in pistol or rifle fights.

Police officers attending the trial identified man after man whose name can be found in the Bertillon records at police headquarters. They were there, from the ordinary silk-shirted maquereaux, the gambler, the pickpocket, the former convict, and many others. Their sympathies and hopes were with Mattie Howard. They were sure she would be found not guilty. The disappointment in the verdict showed more keenly in many of the faces in the courtroom than it did on that of convicted woman.

To the police and to the underworld, she long has been known as the "woman of mystery." The underworld said the police had to "make good" and "stuck" Mattie for Morino's death. The police harked back to the underworld that she either killed Morino or knew who did.

| 10 |

A Foul Odor

"The crowded court room slowly emptied. The throngs of people departed, satisfied that the verdict had been just. Mattie bore it all alone. Not one in the crowd offered her even a sympathetic glance. As an officer led her from the court room, the judge remarked, 'I have been judge here for fifteen years, but she is the most beautiful woman I ever had to sentence.'"

The Pathway of Mattie Howard (To and from Prison): True Story of the Regeneration of an Ex-Convict and Gangster Woman by M. Harris, copyright by Mattie Howard, 1937

D ays after Mattie Howard's conviction, a reporter for *The Post* visited her in the Jackson County Jail. She wore a white house apron as well as the wristwatch, rings, and the gold earrings she had displayed throughout the trial. She had been passing the time in jail sewing and playing cards with her fellow prisoners.

Mattie remained defiant and confident that the appeals would go her way, at which time she would accept the offers made her by motion picture producers.

"The case was a frameup," she said as she leaned against the iron bars of her cell's window and watched people on the street below hurry through the fog.

"I'll admit that I had a little record, and when a person is unfortunate enough to have been brought up before the police, that is the end of it. They will follow up and 'frame' you in every way possible. The case was unfair and partial."

"You seemed very calm during the trial," the reporter said.

"Well, I could have cried during the whole trial, and then people would have said that I was seeking sympathy. I could choose between appearing hard-hearted and weeping, and I chose the former. But that doesn't mean that many sobs were not stifled in my throat."

Actual sobs might have worked better on the twelve male jurors.

But she followed Jesse James Jr.'s instructions "to act cool and to display no emotion," according to *The Pathway of Mattie Howard.* "Her attorney had even supplied her with grapes and peanuts, directing her to chew them in order to appear nonchalant."

The book also accused James of purposely trying to get her convicted so he could earn more money during the appeals. It seems more likely, however, that James's failures were a simple case of poor lawyering.

Then there was the fact that Mattie clearly lied on the witness stand, which probably didn't help her in the eyes of the jury.

When asked whether she had been arrested with gangster Tony Cruye, which was an unquestionable truth, she said no. She denied a series of other easily provable facts, insisted she had nothing to do with any part of Joe Morino's murder, and claimed she had no ties with any of the known criminals she was known to associate with.

Perhaps she shouldn't have tried to come across as a total angel, which she clearly was not. Jury members might have decided that if she was lying about simple, obvious things, she was lying about everything.

Still, the case against Mattie Howard had a foul odor about it — and we're not talking just about the stink that supposedly attracted porter Ira Allen into Apartment 301 at the Touraine Apartment Hotel when he discovered Joe Morino's body early on Saturday, May 25, 1918.

Witnesses changed their stories, prosecutors' theories went unchallenged, and potentially key evidence was ignored.

For example, the science used to determine time of death wasn't as advanced in 1918 as it is now, so deputy coroner J.S. Snider could only speculate about when Morino was killed based on the condition of the body. Snider originally told police and reporters that the murder occurred Friday night, some twelve hours before Allen found the body.

But as police zeroed in on Mattie — who had an alibi for Friday night — Snider changed his time of death to Thursday night. That's what he testified to at trial.

Other witness statements from the early days of the police investigation also conveniently changed or were never mentioned at trial.

Remember Zeffrino Gamba, Morino's clerk, who told police early in the investigation that his boss was infatuated with a big blond woman? And that she was about thirty-five years old? Gamba eventually came around to identifying twenty-three-year-old Mattie.

How about the man staying on the second floor of the Touraine who said he heard "what sounded to be a heavy thud" on the floor above him at about 10 p.m. Friday? He was never heard from again once police and prosecutors settled on Thursday night for the time of the murder.

Even the testimony of M.D. Duval, who had heard suspicious noises from No. 301 on the evening of Thursday, May 23, didn't necessarily contradict a Friday-night time of death. The bailing wire and Morino's multiple wounds suggested an extended period of torture, after all. The noises on Thursday night easily could have resulted from the torture, not the actual killing.

At trial, James never challenged prosecutors when they called the blackjack the murder weapon, even though Snider had determined early in the investigation that it wasn't. And why didn't he at least suggest that the notorious Black Hand gangsters might have been involved in the killing of a fellow Italian? Or point a finger at the since-deceased Dale Jones, a logical suspect if ever there was one?

Finally, why didn't James pound away at the Touraine employees who said they hadn't noticed anything unusual when they entered the apartment where the battered and bloody corpse of Joe Morino supposedly lay all day Friday?

* * *

The case against Mattie appears to have been a setup by the police and prosecution, with assistance from James — either through his cooperation or, more likely, his incompetence.

That doesn't mean she wasn't somehow involved in the murder of Joe Morino.

Based on witness statements that were consistent from start to finish, Mattie likely did accompany Morino to the third-floor room in the Touraine on Wednesday, May 22, 1918. But she almost certainly wasn't in the hotel room when Morino was killed.

So, at best, Mattie Howard was guilty of accessory to murder. More than likely, the police knew as much but built a case against Mattie anyway, expecting her to give up whichever of her gangster buddies were involved in killing Morino.

But she was no rat, a fact that her underworld cronies greatly appreciated.

Chances are the actual killer was Dale Jones who, dressed as a woman, entered the Touraine with Morino and another woman on the fateful evening. Two years after the trial, I.B. Walston, Kansas City's chief of detectives, said police were convinced the "other woman" was Jones dressed in women's clothes.

If so, Mattie would have known that Jones was the killer but kept her mouth shut — even though Jones was dead by the time her trial took place. It's possible he had bought her silence by paying for her defense, and she was committed to covering for him even after his death. Why not? She probably never expected to be convicted and sent to the penitentiary — and the publicity of a trial might turn her into a star.

Perhaps James, the mouthpiece for so many K.C. gangsters, also knew the truth but agreed not to implicate Jones as the likely killer during the trial. Could that be why the jury never heard from the informant who said Jones admitted to killing Morino?

Remember him?

* * *

Mattie Howard was a convicted murderer, but the state penitentiary would have to wait. She was back on the streets of Kansas City within three weeks of her guilty verdict.

At a hearing before Judge Latshaw on November 15, 1919, James sought bail for Mattie pending the hearing of a motion for a new trial. James based the appeal on his claims that assistant county prosecutor Edward J. Curtin had made misleading and prejudicial statements.

I covered the hearing for *The Star*:

"Half a dozen gaily dressed men were interested spectators as the woman was brought from her cell. She came forth smiling, attired in the height of fashion.

"'I'll be out to see you in a little while,' she called to them."

Indeed she was.

Judge Latshaw said he would take the new trial motion under advisement. Meanwhile, Mattie was freed on a $10,000 bond signed by L.C. Talbott, who identified himself as a grocer.

Curtin next set his sights on Sam Taylor.

The same Sam Taylor who was arrested with Mattie in Raton, New Mexico, and like her faced a murder charge in the Morino killing — even though J.L. Ghent, Kansas City's acting chief of police, said within days of the pair's arrest in June 1918 that he believed Taylor was not connected with the murder.

For now, he was in a St. Louis jail, having been convicted in August 1919 of having burglary tools in his possession. He was arrested with Mattie in that case as well.

Curtin said he had proof of Taylor's involvement in Morino's murder. It included an entirely new theory about one of the most important elements of the crime, and it contradicted what he presented at Mattie's trial.

The assistant prosecutor's revised theory suggested that he had been wrong — or lied — during Mattie's trial when he claimed she checked into the Touraine with Morino, supposedly setting him up for his eventual murder. Instead, he now claimed, it was Mattie and Sam Taylor who had portrayed the infamous "B. Stanley and wife, Detroit." Then she lured Morino to the scene, where Taylor killed him.

How convenient for the prosecution.

That updated scenario had a giant hole in it. If it was Taylor who checked into the Touraine with Mattie and who the next night returned with Mattie and another woman, how did Joe Morino wind up in No. 301? If he wasn't "B. Stanley," then Touraine employees never saw him.

Curtin's new theory had no direct bearing on Mattie Howard's fate, of course. She remained a convicted murderer, even if she was free on bond.

The movie producers never came calling, but if you believe the Kansas City police, Mattie spent the next several months playing a role that could easily have been taken from a silent film of that era. They were convinced that she not only was blowing safes and committing other crimes but that she was the brains behind an entire criminal enterprise.

Accordingly, they knocked on her door almost every time a crime was committed.

She said later that she couldn't hold a job because of the police harassment and that her desperation led to excessive drinking (despite the recent start of Prohibition). She said she also turned to shoplifting, an art she had learned during her time in jail.

Finally, Mattie decided to leave Kansas City, getting permission from the court to go to St. Louis, where her sister lived. Alas, Mattie was in jail within twenty-four hours of arriving in the city on the opposite side of Missouri.

Her story was that she visited a jewelry store her first morning in St. Louis to have a ring repaired and, by pure coincidence, that very jewelry store was robbed later in the day. The St. Louis police, knowing Mattie's record, locked her up.

She spent some three months in jail before being released when the robbers were caught with the stolen jewelry. They insisted Mattie had nothing to do with the heist.

She was ordered to return immediately to Kansas City.

By this time, it was early March 1920, and — again if you believe the Kansas City police — Mattie went to work planning perhaps the biggest job of her career. It became a highly publicized event in Kansas City that could only be described as a total and tragic failure.

| 11 |

Pagel's Return

"(Assistant Jackson County prosecutor Edward) Curtin says he has reliable information that Mattie Howard, dressed as a man, accompanies her gang members often. Curtin attributed most of the safe robberies in this vicinity to the gang directed by the woman. 'I have learned,' Curtin said, 'that Mattie can crack a safe as neatly as anyone.'"
The Kansas City Star, March 12, 1920

The South Side Bank at 3838 Main had opened for business at 9 a.m. on Tuesday, March 9, 1920, and tellers, bookkeepers, accountants, and loan officers had barely settled into their desk chairs.

Bank treasurer Maurice J. McNellis was leaning against his desk just inside the entrance, opening mail, and janitor Jim Smith was a few feet away.

The bank was more than two miles south of downtown Kansas City in an area that was just beginning to attract businesses and saw relatively little automobile traffic, making it an inviting target for bank robbers wanting an easy getaway.

The South Side Bank had begun operating barely two years earlier. Within its first three weeks, it was held up, with a single bandit flashing a gun, locking the bank workers in a closet, and taking $3,000. Police suspected members of the Jones-Lewis gang, whom a few months later police would track to a house two blocks from the bank at 3715 Wyandotte after the highly publicized MKT train robbery.

Accordingly, bank employees were vigilant — so much so that some kept pistols within arm's reach.

As McNellis opened his mail, he saw four men wearing overcoats at the door. They didn't cover their faces with masks, but McNellis knew their intentions.

"When I glanced up, I noticed the men were young and each of them appeared to be holding to something in his coat pocket," he said. "I felt it was a holdup and jumped forward to lock the door.

"Before I could lock the door, one or two of the men pushed by me. Then something struck me, and I fell."

Jim Smith, the janitor, also saw the men at the door, and he realized they had revolvers.

Smith heard one yell, "Get him!," meaning McNellis, then saw McNellis fall injured as he lunged toward the entrance. Smith moved to assist the bank treasurer, but he was met by a man who was evidently trying to enter the cashier's cage.

"Then one of them either shot me or bit me," Smith said.

Stenographer Eva Lathrop was in the cashier's cage, just behind cashier Glenn M. Shockey. She said Shockey grabbed his revolver at about the time the would-be robber hollered, "Get him!"

Shockey immediately fired.

"I leaped to my feet, glancing over his shoulder to see at whom he was shooting," the stenographer said. "Then I saw one of the three men shoot. Two of them forced their way inside the railing and were standing at the door leading into Mr. Shockey's cage.

"Both men had revolvers. I saw them and shouted, 'Oh, don't!' and ducked behind the counter. The men fired several times. Mr. Shockey fired once or twice and fell at his feet, his hand clutching his breast.

"'Get a doctor, Miss Lathrop, I'm shot,' was the last he said to any of us."

At this point, the robbers beat a swift retreat, turning back toward the front door without ever announcing their intention or demanding money.

The shooting was far from over, however.

Bookkeeper Henry Strohmeyer rushed from the rear of the bank, emptying his revolver as he followed the four bandits all the way to the street, where a dark gray Cadillac with a driver awaited. The bandits returned fire but didn't hit Strohmeyer.

As the final bandit climbed into the getaway car, a bullet from Strohmeyer's revolver struck him. He collapsed to the ground and his cohorts pulled him into the Cadillac, which sped away north on Main Street.

The bookkeeper continued his pursuit by jumping on a passing streetcar, but his attempt to follow the getaway car was futile. After a few blocks, Strohmeyer left the streetcar and returned to the bank.

But the bandits still weren't in the clear.

As the four would-be robbers had exited the bank, B.B. Pittenger was driving past. The car salesman, behind the wheel of a Ford, saw the exchange of shots between Strohmeyer and the men and quickly surmised what was happening.

Pittenger decided to follow the Cadillac, which meandered nearby streets at a moderate speed, evidently trying to avoid suspicion. North on Main about four blocks to Armour Boulevard, east another four blocks to Gillham Road, north on Gillham yet another four blocks to Thirty-first Street, east briefly to Holmes Street, back south a block to Linwood Boulevard, and east a half-mile or so to The Paseo.

As the Cadillac reached The Paseo, a major north-south artery, one bandit finally noticed the car following them. The driver gunned the Cadillac's powerful engine, and Pittenger couldn't keep up in his Ford. He quickly lost sight of the getaway car as it sped south on The Paseo.

Back at the bank, stenographer Eva Lathrop had briefly left the wounded Glenn Shockey and returned with a doctor. But it was too late. The cashier, who had been hit by four bullets from at least two guns, died within about fifteen minutes. Neighbors had fetched

Shockey's wife from their nearby home, and she was beside her husband when he died.

Lathrop said the attempted robbery left her "rather dazed."

"I have had a premonition that something like this would happen," she said. "Mr. Shockey kept a revolver and always said that if a robber ever came in it would be either he or the robber."

"Did you faint?" she was asked.

"Why should I faint?" she responded. "I was trying to figure out some way to get out."

Shockey had been teaching Lathrop the South Side Bank's bookkeeping system.

"It's a good thing to learn this system, Miss Lathrop," he had told her. "There is no telling when you will be called upon to take my place."

* * *

Police arrested five men within thirty minutes of the attempted robbery, and janitor Jim Smith identified one as having been among the bandits. But it wasn't long before the authorities decided they weren't the perpetrators.

The five, described as youths, were arrested in a Ford sedan, not a Cadillac. None was wearing an overcoat, and none was suffering from a gunshot wound. They were captured with two guns, .38-caliber and .32-caliber revolvers.

Deputy coroner J.S. Snider, the same man who had examined Joe Morino's murder scene almost two years earlier, had hurried to the bank and took two .25-caliber bullets and two .45-caliber bullets from Shockey's body.

Pittenger, the car salesman who had followed the getaway car, provided police with the license-plate number on the Cadillac. But it was listed as belonging on a 1917 Ford.

The Kansas City Star, March 9, 1920

* * *

Two women who lived at 4409 Montgall Avenue, about two miles southeast of where Pittenger had last seen the Cadillac, were expecting out-of-town visitors, so they were keeping watch from the home's front window.

When one of the women saw a dark-colored Cadillac pull up, she called out that "the folks" were arriving. But then she saw a man jump out of the front seat of the Cadillac and run into the house next door at 4405 Montgall. He returned almost immediately to the car.

"He said something, and then two men climbed out of the back seat," the woman said. "Supporting a third man who was in the rear of the seat, they attempted to stand him up. He could not stand."

So the two men picked up their cohort, who was wearing an overcoat, and carried him into the house next door.

"They appeared frightened and glanced about them all the time they were getting the man out. The man being carried had a gray pallor on his face and appeared to be suffering immensely."

The woman said the two men who carried the wounded man into the house exited together and left the scene walking, one to the west and the other to the south. The Cadillac then headed south.

She described the men as in their twenties and neatly dressed in dark clothes. Four of them wore dark felt hats, and the driver wore a cap.

Within about twenty minutes, the vigilant neighbors saw a lone man enter the house next door. A modest three-bedroom house built four years earlier, 4405 Montgall happened to be the residence of James and George Evans, two of Kansas City's most notorious gangsters.

* * *

Dr. Joseph A. Beebe said he was at his home on Eleventh Street when a man called at about 9:45 a.m. Dr. Beebe, who had previously treated the wife of George Evans, said the caller indicated he needed a doctor for "a case of the flu."

Dr. Beebe replied that he didn't treat the flu, but the caller insisted he was needed. He told the doctor to arrange a taxi by calling Main 7500, the number of Blue Cab Company, whose proprietor, Abram Miller, was at the time facing an auto theft charge. In fact, a week later he would be convicted and sentenced to two years, ten months in the state penitentiary. It seems he stole a car, painted it blue, and added it to his fleet of taxis.

The Blue Cab taxi took Dr. Beebe to 4405 Montgall.

"When I got to the house, I found a man there who had been shot in the left hip, the bullet passing through to the right hip," he said. "I gave the man a hypodermic injection and dressed the wound superficially.

"I advised taking him to a hospital for operation, but he opposed it. The women told me he had been shot while in a crap game."

Dr. Beebe was one of many visitors to 4405 Montgall that day, according to the next-door neighbors, who indicated a steady stream of flashily dressed young and middle-aged men, mostly in high-priced cars, came and went.

At some point in the afternoon, the watchful neighbors saw a man with a bandaged arm and an overcoat over his shoulders walk from the Evans house to a waiting car driven by a one-armed man. The car sped away.

In the early evening, a Buick arrived with a second physician — Dr. A.J. Gannon. Three men waited in the car while Dr. Gannon entered the house.

He immediately saw that the waiting patient had already been assisted by another doctor and that he had a gunshot wound, which he was not equipped to treat. A few minutes after his arrival, the neighbor ladies heard the moans of the wounded man.

Finally, at least eight hours after seeing the Cadillac arrive with the wounded man, the neighbors called the police.

* * *

The Woodland Avenue police station received the telephone call detailing the suspicious happenings at 4405 Montgall, and officers sprang into action.

When Sergeant C.M. Larrabee and seven officers armed with riot guns arrived at the house, the unlucky trio of Joseph Burke, Charles B. Johnson, and Walter J. Smith were still sitting out front in the Buick that had delivered Dr. Gannon. Police officers held them at gunpoint while their compatriots entered the house and found Dr. Gannon with the wounded man.

Police made the arrests without gunfire.

In addition to Burke, Johnson, and Smith, the wounded man — who gave his name as James E. Morgan — was arrested. Morgan was taken to General Hospital.

Held as material witnesses were Daisy Evans, wife of George Evans; Lucy Evans, wife of Jim Evans; and Joseph Clevenger, fourteen-year-old nephew of Daisy Evans who was living with the Evans family.

Dr. Gannon, who said that he had been Walter J. Smith's physician for about ten years and that Smith had sought him out to treat a man injured in a crap game, was not charged.

The Evans brothers were not in the house, but police were still one suspect short. Five men, including the driver, had been involved in the South Side Bank attempted robbery, and they had nabbed only four. Police figured they had a lead on their fifth suspect, though, because the neighbor women told them about the man with a bandaged arm leaving the Evans house in a car. The women added a useful detail: The car was driven by a one-armed man.

The four arrested men and the two women gave police a variety of stories, including the assertion by the two Evans wives that Morgan was thrown from a moving car in front of their house and carried inside by two passersby.

"The car from which Morgan was thrown never stopped," Lucy Evans said, "and the two men who carried him into our house left immediately."

Both women denied knowing Morgan, and all the prisoners denied knowledge of the attempted bank robbery. Morgan was especially vehement in insisting he was not involved, telling hospital workers he was wounded during a crap game in the rear of a judge's court room.

An abandoned blue-gray Cadillac with a bullet mark on the right front fender and several bullets in the back seat was found shortly after the arrests not far from the Montgall address. It was later identified as having been stolen two nights earlier.

* * *

By Wednesday, March 10, 1920, one day after the attempted robbery of the South Side Bank that resulted in the shooting death of cashier Glenn M. Shockey, police had no evidence tying Mattie Howard to the crime.

Well, almost none.

They had determined that James E. Morgan was none other than Albert Pagel. The man lying in a hospital bed with a bullet wound in his hip was Mattie's lover.

Police identified Pagel after a detective recognized the man calling himself Morgan as the same man the detective had arrested January 26 using the alias Harry E. Jones. He was accused of blowing the safe at the Globe Theater, but the charges were dismissed because of lack of evidence.

Pagel had been a suspect in many other robberies, the police said. In one case, a detective had received an anonymous letter linking Pagel to a robbery of four cases of liquor that resulted in the killing of a night watchman.

After the police found records of Pagel's stays at the federal penitentiary in Leavenworth and the Missouri state penitentiary, they told reporters of his relationship with Mattie. That revelation returned her to the front pages for the first time since her trial.

Under the headline "Morgan a 'Pal' of Mattie's," I wrote how she had supplied money for Pagel's trial in Springfield and how he had furnished funds for her trial in Kansas City. I also reported that Mattie had visited Pagel, who was being held in a barred-cell hospital room, shortly after he arrived at General Hospital.

Robert E. Phelan, chief of detectives, told me he was convinced that Mattie served as the mastermind behind many recent crimes in Kansas City and throughout the region. "Crimes that bore the trademark of the woman's genius for detail and organization have baffled Robert E. Phelan, chief of detectives," I wrote. "He believed he saw the work of Mattie Howard's hand, but was seen through a mist. No trails from blown safes led to her door."

These crimes, it's worth noting, took place while Mattie was free on bail, either awaiting trial for murder or awaiting her appeal after being convicted of murder.

Curtin theorized that Mattie planned the South Side Bank robbery to obtain funds for the defense of Sam Taylor in his upcoming trial for the murder of Joe Morino. Curtin, who was prosecuting Taylor, explained that underworld characters pulled bank jobs and other crimes to collect "fall money" to pay each other's bondsmen, lawyers, and "fixers."

In his hospital bed, Pagel required help of another kind.

Doctors, with police officials present, operated on him to remove the bullet from his hip. The wounded bandit, who was conscious for the operation, asked to see the bullet. When an attendant handed it to Pagel, he tried to swallow it. The attendants thwarted his effort.

The bullet proved to be .44-caliber, same as the revolver of bank bookkeeper Henry Strohmeyer, who fired at the fleeing bandits.

* * *

Also on March 10, Strohmeyer, bank stenographer Eva Lathrop, and Dr. E.B. Riley, a dentist with offices above the South Side Bank, paid a visit to Pagel's hospital room. None identified him as having been involved in the attempted holdup.

"I did not get a good look at the man's face yesterday," Strohmeyer said.

"I cannot identify this man," Lathrop said.

The three witnesses were taken to police headquarters, where they did no better in identifying the three other suspects.

"I do not recall the men in the bank," Lathrop said.

Makes you wonder whether the stenographer and the others, with a day to consider the potential danger of pointing the finger at members of the underworld, developed cases of the same amnesia that plagued so many witnesses to Kansas City crimes of that era.

It turned out that one of the arrested men, Charles B. Johnson, had a background almost as colorful as Pagel/Morgan. Police determined that Johnson was, in fact, Frank McFarland and was wanted in Minneapolis on a car theft charge. He was also known by the aliases George Conkin, Arthur McMahon, and "Memphis Kid."

Meanwhile, detectives had a surprise visitor Wednesday: James Evans, one of the two brothers whose home the would-be bank robbers fled to after the previous day's botched holdup. He arrived with a lawyer in tow.

"I don't know a thing about the trouble," Evans told chief of detectives Phelan. "I've been out on a drunk. I learned about it today when I read the papers."

Evans was asked if he knew where his brother George was.

"I don't know," he replied. "He's been drinking heavily for the last few days. I'm sure he didn't have anything to do with it. He'll probably come to his senses and give himself up tomorrow."

So there you have it: the birth of the we-were-too-drunk-to-have-done-it alibi.

* * *

You wouldn't think a bullet in the hip was a life-threatening injury, but by Thursday evening, March 11, 1920, it was clear Pagel's wound was in fact serious.

Mattie called the hospital repeatedly as the night progressed to get updates on her lover's condition. Shortly before midnight, hospital officials told her Pagel was worsening, and she jumped in a car and headed for the hospital.

Wearing a long leather coat, she arrived at General Hospital within about fifteen minutes and asked to see Pagel. When she reached his hospital cell room, she attempted to enter the barred doorway, but hospital employees stopped her. They said she had to talk to Pagel through the iron gratings.

Pagel raised his head from his cot when he heard Mattie's voice.

"I knew you'd come, darling," he said.

"Hello, sweetheart," she replied.

"Come on in, Mattie dear, and rub my forehead," Pagel said.

She again pleaded with hospital workers to let her enter the room, but they refused.

"I wired your sister in Brooklyn," she said. "Everything is all right."

She saw that Pagel was fading.

"Do you know you are going to die?"

He nodded yes.

"Are you afraid to die?"

"Promise me you will always be a good girl."

"I will be good."

After their brief encounter, Mattie was led to a bench in the hospital corridor to await her lover's fate.

* * *

While Mattie was waiting, chief of detectives Phelan led twelve officers armed with riot guns and revolvers into a rooming house on East Fourteenth street in the wee morning hours of Friday, March 12. They rushed into a room and roused a sleeping man.

"Don't shoot," the man squealed. "You've got me."

"Yes, you are one of the birds that held up the bank the other day," Phelan said to him.

"Yes, I'm the guy. But don't shoot. I'll tell you all about it," the man replied.

The officers threw a bed quilt around the man, who was suffering from bullet wounds in his left arm, neck, and back. He was taken to police headquarters.

Police identified him as Edmond J. Hart and were confident he was the injured man the neighbors had seen leave the Evans house Tuesday afternoon, driven away by a one-armed man.

He admitted that — and much more.

Hart was taken to police headquarters, where he made a detailed confession to Phelan. He said he was involved in the attempted bank robbery and was shot during the getaway, although he insisted he didn't know he was getting involved in a holdup when he agreed to accompany several men that morning. He also refused to implicate any others.

He admitted he was wanted in Minneapolis for bank robbery and said his alias was Ed Neary.

After confessing, Hart was taken to the Westport police station, where his guard was L.A. Myers. By happenstance, Myers had worked with Hart as brakemen for a railroad.

"Well, Lou, I'm glad the thing is over," Hart told Myers.

"Why, Ed?"

"Well, I just been thinking of all the mean things I have done in my life and all the good things, and I think most of them are mean. I'll be through for a while, anyway."

Later Friday, police also nabbed William Thompson, a twenty-nine-year-old, one-armed taxi driver. He was identified by the observant neighbors of the Evans brothers as the man who chauffeured the injured Hart that fateful Tuesday. He confessed as much to the police.

* * *

After the police captured Hart and heard his story, detectives William Doarn and T.J. Foley paid Pagel a visit at General Hospital — with Mattie still waiting in the corridor.

"Morgan, you're going to kick off," Doarn said.

"Is that so?"

"Have you anything to say?"

"Nothing. I want to be left alone," Pagel said. "I don't want any doctors or anyone else in here. And don't notify anybody. But I want people kept from running in and out of this room. If I'm going to die, I want to die in peace."

* * *

At about 4 a.m., Dr. G.F. Cummins told Mattie that Pagel had died.

She screamed uncontrollably before begging to see him. Once in the room, she put her arms around Pagel's head and wept.

She left the hospital shortly after 6 a.m. with her attorney, Jesse James, after telling officials to take the body to an undertaker, indicating she would pay for his funeral expenses.

| 12 |

'Damn those coppers!'

"The glint of defiance is gone from those agate eyes, and in its stead is the gleam of tears. A heart called stone has melted. Yesterday, Mattie Howard, from her throne in the underworld, buried a challenge. Today she is conquered. Albert Pagel, her sweetheart, is dead, and with him all that she held dear. Mattie Howard is a broke, desolate woman."
The Kansas City Star, March 13, 1920

Mattie Howard certainly appeared to be broke and desolate. Gone was the stoicism she displayed in the courtroom during her murder trial. In its place came torrents of tears and howls of anguish.

Had she really undergone a sudden transformation, or might she have been putting on an act in an effort to rebuild her public image?

In any case, the Mattie Howard death march now included gangster friends Dale Jones, Frank Lewis, Blackie Lancaster, Tony Cruye, and Albert Pagel, all of whom had died during or after shootouts and all within eighteen months.

Still, the woman who had been convicted of second-degree murder in October 1919 remained a free woman in March 1920, and she would be free for many months to come. She also remained a popular topic for me and my fellow Kansas City reporters, who tracked her every move.

First at the Carroll & Mast undertaking establishment, then at Pagel's funeral and burial, and finally at her court appearance for a hearing on a possible new trial — all in less than a week. At the same time, her name continued to be bandied about in connection with the South Side Bank robbery attempt a few days earlier that had left Pagel and cashier Glenn M. Shockey dead.

* * *

Mattie arrived at Carroll & Mast at about 8 p.m. March 12, some sixteen hours after her lover's death. Accompanied by three women, she was there to arrange for the funeral of Albert Pagel.

"Albert!" she screamed as she entered the building. "Albert!"

She remained hysterical despite the efforts of her companions and the undertaker to comfort her. Demanding to see Pagel's body and pulling away from those trying to pacify her, the sobbing woman burst into the room where the corpse lay on a marble slab.

"I know what they did to you, honey!" she squealed. "I know how they killed you in that cage. They got you, and they can get me the same way. You just wait and see."

Mattie then collapsed, with her blond hair draped across her lover's dead body, before being revived. One of her companions called Jesse James Jr. on the telephone.

"We haven't been able to do anything with her since he died," the woman told James. "She has screamed for hours. After all, she's a woman."

A few minutes later, her companions ushered Mattie to a waiting car even though the funeral details had not been arranged.

"I can't leave him," she said as they pushed her into the car.

The next day, she appeared at General Hospital to retrieve Pagel's belongings but found only his blood-stained clothing. She clutched them and wept once more before returning to the undertaker, where Mattie, dressed in black and her face hidden by a veil, kept vigil at the corpse's side almost constantly until Pagel's funeral two days later. (At this point, it's worth remembering Mattie was still legally married to another man.)

On the same day, as the five people charged as accessories after the fact in the murder and attempted robbery at the South Side Bank arrived at the Jackson County Criminal Court for their arraignment before our friend Judge Ralph S. Latshaw, heavily armed police guarded the entrances and officers with rifles stood poised in the streets. All pleaded not guilty.

The Post pointed out that "Mattie Howard, the vampire woman with the 'agate eyes,' did not appear at the hearing" on March 13.

It also reported: "Unless further evidence is obtained to prove that Mattie Howard planned and supervised the attempted robbery of the bank in which two lives were lost, no action against her will be taken." Police believed that "the principals in the bandit organization have been brought to justice" in the case.

* * *

Underworld characters and police detectives were among the crowd that crammed into the Carroll & Mast undertaking establishment in the late afternoon of March 16 for the funeral of Albert Pagel. The private service attracted too many interested parties for the small chapel to hold, and the overflow filled the hallway outside.

Men and women waited in line to glimpse the dead criminal in his casket, but none shed any tears. Those were reserved for Mattie.

She reportedly paid for the funeral, complete with a full array of flowers, although it is hard to fathom how the unemployed convicted murderer could afford to do so. She also selected hymns and Bible passages for the service.

Gladys Arthur of the First Baptist Church sang "Does Jesus Care?" and "In the Sweet By and By."

A troop of pallbearers consisting of underworld characters lugged the coffin to a gray hearse, and Mattie sobbed her way to a limousine before the seven-vehicle funeral procession made its way to Elmwood Cemetery. After arriving, Mattie sang softly as Albert Pagel's gangster associates carried him to his grave, where hundreds of curiosity seekers were among those who watched the burial.

Mattie sobbed as her lover's body was lowered into the grave.

Hours later, after the crowd had left, attendants at the cemetery spotted the black-clad woman still at Pagel's grave.

"My heart lies buried there," she screamed. "Damn those coppers!"

* * *

Still out on a $10,000 bond, Mattie was scheduled to head back to Judge Ralph S. Latshaw's courtroom March 19 for a hearing on James's motion for a new trial. The day before the hearing, assistant prosecutor Edward Curtin made it clear he would show no mercy.

"Mattie Howard is having a bad effect on the community," Curtin said. "Her association with Albert Pagel, killed in the South Side Bank robbery, convinces me she still is active in criminal circles."

At the hearing itself, Curtin went even further.

After Mattie entered the courtroom supported by a female friend and a nurse outfitted in a white cap and apron, Curtin pointed his finger at the defendant and went on a verbal rampage.

"There sits one of the most dangerous women in the community. Every man she ever associated with either is dead, in the penitentiary, or awaiting trial for some crime.

"There's 'Blackie' Lancaster, Dale Jones, Albert Pagel, Tony Cruye — her friends — all dead criminals. Poor Joe Morino, the pawnbroker, lies in his grave, lured to his death in the Touraine Apartment Hotel by Mattie Howard. She's responsible for the death of two men and the wounding of another in the recent robbery of the South Side Bank. I'm going to do my best to rid the community of such a woman!"

Latshaw gave Mattie the chance to plead her own case.

"Judge, I'm not guilty of killing Joe Morino," she said as tears rolled down her cheeks.

"Twelve better men than I have decided on your guilt," Judge Latshaw said.

"All that's said about me isn't true, judge," she insisted, burying her face in her arms and sobbing.

The tears didn't keep Latshaw from denying the motion for a new trial, although Mattie did gain one small victory. Latshaw decided she would not have to go to the penitentiary until the Missouri Supreme Court ruled on her appeal.

So Mattie remained free on bond.

* * *

Within two months, two more of Mattie's criminal associates went down — Charles "Spider" Kelly and Sam Taylor.

Taylor was the lucky one. He got life in prison.

Kelly had been arrested with Mattie and Tony Cruye on July 24, 1919, in conjunction with the robbery of a safe in the National Reserve Bank Building, but charges were dropped against all involved. He also had been with Cruye a few weeks later when their attempt to rob a high-stakes poker game resulted in the shooting death of Cruye.

In January 1920, Kelly was arrested after a shooting at a whorehouse but was released when the victim survived and declined to prosecute.

Then it was Kelly's turn to catch a bullet, and his was fatal. He was shot when he and two other men tried to rob a drugstore. He died April 9, 1920.

Meanwhile, Taylor, who had been arrested with Mattie for the killing of Morino, waited for his murder trial in the Jackson County Jail, where Mattie was known to visit him. In late April, jailers found a steel saw in Taylor's cell, as well as nitroglycerin and more equipment in other cells. They determined that Taylor and two other inmates had been on the verge of making an escape attempt.

The jailers might have suspected that Mattie had smuggled in the contraband, because they immediately outlawed visitors.

Taylor would leave his jail cell a few weeks later — but not for freedom.

His trial in May 1920, two years after Morino's death, followed a script similar to Mattie's trial seven months earlier. Ralph S. Latshaw again was the judge, Edward J. Curtin again prosecuted, and Jesse James Jr. again was the defense attorney.

Most of the witnesses were the same, including cab driver Richard Hauer. He identified Taylor as the man he picked up with two women — one of them Mattie Howard — outside the Touraine apartments early on the morning of Friday, May 24, 1918, about thirty hours before Morino's body was found in the Touraine. Taylor and Mattie claimed to be in Picher, Oklahoma, at the time.

Just as in Mattie's trial, virtually all the evidence against Taylor was circumstantial.

One difference was the testimony of George Stewart, another prisoner in the county jail. Stewart testified that he heard Taylor make incriminating comments, among them, "I'm not afraid of Mattie. She'll stand pat."

Another difference was that James made no attempt to establish an alibi for Taylor and, in fact, offered no defense at all.

He evidently didn't even challenge Curtin's convenient change in theory about one of the most important elements of the crime. At Mattie's trial, he claimed she and Morino had checked into the Touraine together as "B. Stanley and wife, Detroit." At Taylor's trial, he said that Mattie and Sam had been "B. Stanley and wife" and that she had lured Morino to No. 301, where Taylor killed him.

This was James's last big murder trial before he gave up lawyering to start making movies, so perhaps he was distracted. Or maybe he was in over his head, as he had been at so many previous murder trials.

In any case, the jury needed only two hours to decide that Taylor was guilty and should serve life at the state penitentiary in Jefferson City. The verdict came on May 19, 1920.

Mattie was not on hand to support her partner in crime, though she insisted in later years that Taylor had nothing to do with Morino's murder. Of course, the only way she could know Taylor wasn't involved was if she had been involved herself — or at least knew who the real killer was.

* * *

By the time Taylor ambled off to the state pen, Mattie had begun her own year-and-a-half sojourn.

Given the chaos in her criminal and personal life, it made sense that she might be susceptible to an effort to recruit her away from the dark side. And sure enough, a Christian woman knocked at her door.

Mrs. Frank Gladman had been reading about Mattie's travails and praying for the wayward young woman. Now she planned to help.

"I want you to come home with me," Mrs. Gladman said, standing outside Mattie's closed door because the convicted murderer refused to open it for the stranger.

"Go on away. Don't bother me!" Mattie yelled.

The woman continued talking, however, pitching religious mumbo jumbo that only served to infuriate Mattie further. After a bit, Mrs. Gladman fell silent, and Mattie couldn't resist opening the door to see whether her persistent visitor had left.

She found the woman kneeling, silently praying. Before Mattie could close the door and escape back inside her room, Mrs. Gladman darted past her and resumed her pleading and praying.

"Oh, Lord, make her listen to me. Lord, make her listen to me."

Exasperated, Mattie finally gave in.

"If it will shut you up, woman, all right I'll go with you."

And so she did, taking up residence with Mr. and Mrs. Frank Gladman. Mattie appreciated the kindness of the two but not their constant religious badgering. They were more extreme even than Mattie's mother.

She frequently heard the woman and her husband in their bedroom at night carrying on — not sexually but spiritually — and considered it pure foolishness. Mattie thought they were borderline insane.

She did notice that Mrs. Gladman's prayers tended to be answered, however, so Mattie didn't mind listening to the woman's pleadings to the Lord in one instance.

A telegram arrived telling Mattie that her younger sister had fallen critically ill and wanted Mattie at her bedside at her mother's home in Raton, New Mexico. But would court officials let her leave Kansas City? Not likely, Mattie thought.

After Mrs. Gladman went to her knees and pleaded with the Lord, she said to Mattie, "You will get to go home, and your sister will not die, either."

Sure enough. Authorities not only allowed Mattie to travel to Raton, where her sister did recover, but they also granted her permission to remain there indefinitely.

Did this good fortune that came her way, just as the redoubtably religious Mrs. Gladman assured her it would, convince Mattie to redirect her course in life to a pathway along the straight and narrow? To leave crime and the evils of temptation behind? To dedicate her life to the Lord?

In a word: No.

Not by a long shot.

Instead, Mattie took off for Mexico, where she rediscovered the joys of nightlife and resumed her criminal ways. *The Pathway of Mattie Howard* said she "proved to be far more extreme in her conduct than in former days. ... She became the life of the party."

It was a long party, one that stretched from Mexico to Chicago to Memphis, with rumors of other stops along the way.

After leaving Kansas City in the spring of 1920 to see her sister in Raton, Mattie — as far as can be surmised — didn't step foot in Missouri again until November 1921. She remained a convicted murderer free on bond all that time.

Court and police officials in Kansas City had little idea where she was, but they didn't seem to care much until May 25, 1921. That's when the Missouri Supreme Court finally denied Mattie's appeal. Her $10,000 bond was revoked, and her arrest was ordered so she could be sent immediately to the Missouri penitentiary to serve her twelve-year sentence.

For the second time in three years, Mattie was a wanted woman. Jackson County deputies and Kansas City police began searching for her. But unlike in the aftermath of Joe Morino's murder, tracking her down this time would be neither quick nor easy.

| 13 |

On the Run

"I know I have been dealt with unfairly not only in my trial but other ways. I am not the first one to be punished for something I did not do."
Mattie Howard, statement to the public, November 1921

B y the time the Missouri Supreme Court denied Mattie Howard's appeal and ordered her to prison, much had changed in her world.

The big news during the year since Sam Taylor's murder conviction and her departure for Raton, New Mexico, was that Mattie had become a single woman.

Her divorce from Frank J. Vanders, whom she had married at the age of seventeen in 1912 and had left for the bright lights of Kansas City about five years later, was finalized on September 21, 1920, more than two years after proceedings had begun.

Mattie also had lost her lawyer.

Jesse James Jr. abandoned his law practice to make two silent movies in which he played his father, *Jesse James as the Outlaw* and *Jesse James Under the Black Flag.* Both premiered in early 1921 to largely unimpressed audiences.

Jesse E. James, better known as Jesse James Jr., starred as his father in two movies.
Missouri Valley Special Collections, Kansas City Public Library, Kansas City, Missouri

Meanwhile, one more gangster in Mattie's orbit met a bloody demise.

George Evans was shot and killed on December 15, 1920, while attempting to rob a house of prostitution. Evans had been out on bond pending his trial for accessory to murder in the March 1920 killing of cashier Glenn M. Shockey during the failed South Side Bank robbery that left Albert Pagel mortally wounded. Pagel, bleeding from a gunshot to his hip, had been taken to Evans's house immediately after the robbery attempt, which police suspected Mattie had helped plan.

Now her husband, lawyer, and yet another criminal associate were out of the picture, joining her dead running mates Dale Jones, Frank Lewis, Blackie Lancaster, Tony Cruye, Spider Kelly, and Pagel — to say nothing of Sam Taylor, who was serving life in prison.

But Mattie must have found aid and comfort — if not romance — elsewhere.

For nearly six months after the Supreme Court ruling, she remained at least one step ahead of the law. Reports indicated she had been spotted in Mexico, Canada, Colorado, Des Moines, Cincinnati, Cleveland, Minneapolis, Chicago, Memphis, and Baltimore, but the police couldn't corral her.

She also had hoodwinked her bondsmen, James and grocer Lester Talbott. Before departing for Raton, she gave them a key to a bank safety deposit box she said contained diamonds and bonds that would cover her $10,000 bond. But when the bondsmen's representative inspected the box, all he found were coal, iron washers, and sticks.

At about the same time, the bondsmen received letters from Mattie postmarked Raton, New Mexico, pledging she would return to Kansas City when the Missouri Supreme Court announced its decision. Rightly suspicious, James and Talbott hired a detective. He went to Raton, where he discovered that Mattie's letters had originated elsewhere and had been remailed from Raton. But no sign of Mattie.

Indications were that the letters were mailed originally in the north-central United States, near the Canadian border. So it was believable when newspapers reported on June 2, 1921, that Mattie had been arrested on a fraud charge in Winnipeg, Canada.

An article in *The Kansas City Kansan* said "a 'Mamie' Howard was basking in the police limelight in that city on a charge of 'fraud.' ... A search of her effects had revealed information she undoubtedly was 'the girl with the agate eyes' for whom the Kansas City police have been hunting."

After Kansas City police received a description of Winnipeg's Mamie Howard a few days later, they realized she was not Mattie Howard — but she evidently was a fan. Mamie Howard's personal effects included letters addressed to Mattie.

The tale of Mamie Howard was the first of a series of false sightings and inaccurate reporting, including my own misguided claim that Mattie had been married two months earlier to "a man named either Charles or George Wray, known as 'Corn Bread,'" who was a known criminal.

A month later, newspaper stories said Mattie had been arrested in Chicago by police investigating the theft of a car. Chicago was one place Mattie definitely spent at least part of her time on the lam — she said so herself a few years later — so her possible arrest there made sense.

But, again, the report proved false.

In July 1921, the Mattie tour moved to Memphis, where another Howard woman was arrested and invoked Mattie's name to reporters.

Gladys Marie Howard, a known diamond thief in the South, previously lived in Kansas City and knew all the details of the Joe Morino murder case. Police in Memphis forwarded her records to their Kansas City counterparts, wondering whether there was a Mattie Howard connection. They alleged Gladys had stolen a diamond from a department store by switching it with a fake and then swallowing the real gem.

"They don't want me for the Joe Morino job in Kansas City," she said. "Mattie Howard is the woman who put that diamond broker to sleep, and she is a blond. I'm a brunette. See my dark chestnut hair."

The Birmingham News quoted Gladys Marie Howard as saying, "No, I will never be convicted of this charge. ... I'll vamp them. You see, these Southern gentlemen are so sentimental and soft-hearted it will be an easy matter for me to win them over with my eyes."

Too bad Gladys hadn't been around to coach Mattie at her trial.

* * *

In late October, the Kansas City police issued a reward and a wanted poster — the second of Mattie's relatively brief criminal career. Her value had dropped by half, however, from $1,000 in June 1918 to $500 in the fall of 1921. Joe Morino's estate had offered the earlier reward; Talbott and James, the bondsmen, were responsible for the latter one.

The 1921 poster read: "She will be found with bank robbers, post office robbers and smugglers. Often goes out on the job dressed as a man and may be now disguised as such. She is a leader and planner of the most dangerous type. Would not hesitate to commit murder at any time. May now have her hair auburn or any other color. Natural color is dark blonde."

Scientific American ran a story on the wanted woman's reward and described her as "physically perfect and seemingly mentally acute. She dresses well and makes a good appearance."

The *Baltimore Sun* reported on October 22, 1921, that Mattie was believed to be in Baltimore, that her reward poster hung at the city's police headquarters, and that every patrolman was furnished with her description.

The article read: "She is known to the police of both continents and is said to be wanted for murder, bank robbing, and many minor offenses. She is called the brains of many notorious gangs in the country."

If she really was in Baltimore, Mattie evaded capture once again.

She wasn't so lucky a few weeks later.

* * *

During the late night of November 15, 1921, Memphis police wired Kansas City authorities: "Have in custody Mattie Howard, alias Mrs. Frank J. Vanders, etc., your number 8639. Wire advice at once and send duly authenticated information of indictment and warrant."

That "8639" indicated Mattie's case number at the Kansas City Police Department.

Given the previous similar reports that proved to be wild goose chases, the Kansas City police were understandably wary. "Until we see

Mattie Howard, we'll not believe we have her," said W.D. Crosswhite, acting night chief of detectives.

Still, Crosswhite decided to send officers to Memphis. After all, Mattie's recent fugitive escapades had embarrassed the Kansas City police, and recapturing her would be a big deal.

"The Howard case probably was the most sensational underworld killing ever committed in Kansas City," *The Post* said in a story on November 16. "Mattie Howard was a woman of the underworld. Her love was for hire. Men of wealth and position sought her company. The underworld dueled for her hand."

My story was no less colorful:

"For months (prison) has been waiting to swallow her, with one gulp to take her clean out of the domain of banditry, of which she has been a purported ruler. ... Once she safely is made a morsel for a prison gullet, her game of slipping through the fingers at the end of the law's long arm will be ended."

Now, it appeared the long arm might finally get its hands on her.

Jackson County Prosecuting Attorney Cameron L. Orr began to prepare extradition papers, but then he received word that Mattie had waived extradition. Although she told Memphis detectives she was innocent, she also consented to return to Kansas City as soon as the police there provided an escort.

"I am going back to Kansas City without a struggle," she told police.

Complicating matters, however, was the fact that the grocer/bondsman Talbott had been arrested in Kansas City on a warrant from Des Moines, Iowa, that connected him to a mid-summer bank holdup there.

Three unmasked bandits wielding pistols had robbed the Drake Park Bank of $7,000 in cash and bonds, locking bank employees and customers in the vault before speeding away in a high-powered car. Talbott, who with James had provided Mattie's bond and then forfeited it when she went on the lam, was accused of larceny and receiving stolen property.

He smelled a frame-up.

"I have information Mattie Howard was implicated in that holdup and 'framed' on me to get even because I am seeking to bring about her arrest now," Talbott said.

He said that Mattie and a cohort were in Des Moines but left just after the bank robbery. The grocer/bondsman also was ready to provide fifty-three affidavits proving he was in Kansas City at the time of the Des Moines holdup.

Des Moines officials quickly dropped the charges against Talbott, and Kansas City officials released him just in time for Talbott to travel to Memphis with two deputy marshals, whose superior had been advised them to consider Mattie a dangerous criminal and to keep handcuffs and shackles on her.

* * *

Memphis police said they had kept Mattie and a male companion under surveillance since they arrived from Louisville, Kentucky. When they were involved in a quarrel in front of the Chisca Hotel at Linden and Main streets, police arrested them and took them into custody. Mattie insisted on riding to the police station in a taxicab.

Her companion was J.W. Stevens, known to the Memphis police as an international narcotics runner. He was in possession of more than a pound of cocaine.

Mattie remained calm during questioning, admitting that she was a fugitive and that she was aware of the $500 reward on her head. She told the Memphis police she had permission to be away from Kansas City but would return anyway.

At least, that was the newspaper version of Mattie's capture.

Her own account differed significantly. She outlined it in a handwritten confession of sorts in pocket-sized date book titled *Diary for the Bar of Jackson County, Mo., and Wyandotte County, Kans.* The date book evidently belonged to Talbott, because the expenses and itinerary for his trip to Memphis were noted in the back.

The eighteen pages of longhand writing in pencil began with:

Mattie Howard statement

To the public

I am asking that at least one true story of my trouble and myself be printed for the benefit of myself and those who at this time think me a "Terror."

She then declared her innocence and indicated she was writing a book in which she would explain everything.

So let us start to do that which is right by telling the truth of my arrest in Memphis, Tenn.

First of all I was a new arrival in the city. I got in there I think the time was 8:40 a.m. on the 15ᵗʰ day of Nov. I checked my grip and carelessly walked up town. I knew a girl there whom I met in K.C. Mo. before I ever got in any trouble and she married a Diggs Nolan in Tulsa, Okla., later. I tried to locate her and was directed to Diggs Nolans Drug store in Memphis, Tenn.

Mattie wrote that she had been in Cleveland enjoying the horse races, where she won some money and met "an old gentleman" who owned horses. They got together again in Memphis. The man accompanied Mattie to Diggs Nolan's drugstore, but instead of finding her friend, they found only Nolan, who tried to sell them a fur coat. After a few minutes, they walked out of the drugstore.

The police were waiting.

The whole thing was arranged with Diggs Nolan and his brother to have me arrested but protect themselves if they could. So knowing the old gentleman had money in his pocket Diggs had the officer arrest the old gentleman.

Mattie accompanied the old gentleman to the police station, where she was arrested after being double-crossed by Diggs, who ratted her out to an Inspector Griffin.

He did not have to make any inquiries as to who I was because I told him frankly I was Mattie Howard and was on a $10,000 bond out of Jackson County, Mo.

I told him I was ready to go back — at once waived extradition that night. I did not register at any Hotel there in Memphis, Tenn. I was not quarreling in front of a Hotel. And I was not arrested with any one with dope or anything else in their possession that I know of.

Her statement to the public went on to complain of her unfair treatment and to deny she ever knew, much less was involved with, gangsters Dale Jones and Blackie Lancaster.

The above is true but much could be added to it, however my time for this is limited as I am close to that new home of mine Jefferson Prison.

Still I can't feel it is going to be so terrible. If I was guilty I don't think I could endure it. But God is my judge and he has a reason for putting me to this test and experience.

I regret nothing only that my dear old mother must face this and so far away.

After thanking Talbott — calling him "an honorable man" — and others, including the wife of Jesse James Jr., she closed with:

My request and wish is that if a newspaper exists that will print the truth let me see this in print.

Thank you. I am Miss Mattie Howard.

Her words never made it into any newspapers.

* * *

Mattie provided yet another version of her capture in *The Pathway of Mattie Howard,* likely the book she mentioned she was writing, saying she went to Memphis intending to make her way from there to Kansas City to surrender to authorities. According to the book, Mattie sang to other prisoners in the Memphis jail and her voice was so beautiful that people passing outside the building stopped to listen.

But for Mattie, it finally was time to face the music.

Talbott and the two deputy marshals were to escort her back to Missouri, where twelve years at one of the nation's most notorious prisons awaited.

Before leaving, Talbott sent *The Star* a telegram reading, "Mattie Howard in custody; leaving for Kansas City tonight. Says she was glad to see me." The grocer/bondsman evidently forgave and forgot regarding his accusations a few days earlier that Mattie had framed him for the Des Moines bank robbery.

Jackson County officials originally planned to take Mattie to Kansas City. To avoid any chance her outlaw friends there might attempt to free her, they decided to ship her directly to Jefferson City. That required a rail trip from Memphis to St. Louis, where Talbott, the two deputy marshals, and Mattie would switch trains for the final leg to Jefferson City.

During the stop in St. Louis, Mattie, who apparently had authored her eighteen-page memorandum during the Memphis-to-St. Louis leg of the journey, talked her escorts into letting her send a telegram to her mother in New Mexico.

Hampered by shackles on her ankles and handcuffs on her wrists, she trudged behind the officers to the St. Louis station's telegraph office as fellow travelers stared. With the handcuffs still on, she wrote a note to be transmitted to her mother:

"When you receive this my address will be Box forty-seven Jefferson City Missouri."

That address belonged to the Missouri State Penitentiary. With its imposing limestone walls and sixteen guard towers, the prison was called "The Walls." Sitting mere yards from the southern bank of the Missouri River, it had been operating since 1836.

Mattie Howard arrived at its gates at about 3 p.m. November 18, 1921, seven days after her twenty-seventh birthday, to begin her twelve-year sentence for the murder of Joe Morino.

| 14 |

Convict 24265

"Prison doors closed recently on Mattie Howard, the most remarkable woman of the underworld in the history of Kansas City. ... She appears to be a type more commonly met in the 'movies' than in real life."
Wire story that ran in newspapers nationwide in 1922

Upon arriving at the Missouri Penitentiary, Mattie Howard was led to the administration building, where she met head matron Lila Smith — and immediately provoked the woman who would oversee her in the prison by refusing to do as she ordered.

"When I arrived at the prison, the matron, leering at me, said, 'Well, you eel, we've got you where we want you at last,'" Mattie said years later. "'Believe me, this is one woman you won't fool and one place where you will only be one of many. Just a number.'"

That number was 24265, and Convict 24265 would proceed to defy virtually every order she was given, disregard every prison rule, and resist every person in authority.

She antagonized a Black female trustee who told her to strip for a search and a bath, hissing, "Don't you dare touch me."

She spoke when told to be silent and refused to eat. She set fire to her mattress. She threw a cold-cream jar through a window to let fresh air into her cell and poured dirt down her toilet to clog the plumbing. She hurled scissors at the matron.

Mattie Howard "is probably the most difficult prisoner in the state penitentiary to control," I wrote. "She is strong willed and stubborn. When she does not have her own way, prison officials say she screams at the top of her voice and exhibits a brand of temperament which would cause the envy of a grand opera star."

Because of her notoriety, Mattie also was something of a celebrity in the prison. Whenever Matron Smith led visitors on tours of the women's cells, she always made sure to point out Mattie Howard.

* * *

The women's cell block, separated within the penitentiary grounds from the men's cells by a twenty-foot wall, housed sixty to seventy inmates. Mattie's seven-foot-by-eight-foot cell was on the bottom of four tiers, its walls and ceiling of solid steel. It was adorned with a small table, stool, toilet, sink, and a bunk with a straw-filled mattress.

It was a spartan existence, but at least she had company — roaches, rats, mice, bedbugs, and other vermin.

Perhaps these unwanted cellmates inspired Mattie to fabricate a tale in the hopes of gaining an early release. Within four weeks of her arrival in Jefferson City, she told prison officials she was having fainting spells and refused to work or even leave her bed. Officials sent her meals to her cell.

Newspapers reported that "Missouri's most notorious woman prisoner" insisted she was pregnant, telling Warden Samuel Hill that she had gotten married after her conviction and before her incarceration. The state was known to parole pregnant women to avoid births behind bars.

Mattie wasn't really married, however, and her alleged pregnancy didn't produce a baby or an early release.

At about the same time, Mattie's name surfaced during a sensational murder trial in Kansas.

W.A. Nixon, a respected physician, was accused of killing lawyer Arthur C. Banta, whose body riddled with six gunshots was found beside a country road in July 1921. The prosecution at the trial in Great Bend, Kansas, not only claimed Nixon had shot Banta but that he also was involved in a crime ring with Banta along with known criminals Curly Wallace and Roy Hayes.

On the day Nixon was to testify, his lawyer, Carr W. Taylor, received a note — handwritten in pencil on wrapping paper — that read:

Mattie Howard can tell you who killed Banta at Great Bend, Kan. She and Dago Mike delivered 15 cases of whiskey to Banta that night. Hayes and Wallace killed Banta for the whiskey. Mattie is in pen at Jefferson City. She will talk. Wallace and Hayes tried to hold him up and get the money and whiskey both. Banta knew them and they killed him and stole his whiskey. Save an innocent man.

ONE WHO KNOWS.

Taylor said "if Mattie Howard has any important knowledge of the killing, application will be made to the court for the introduction of her testimony."

That never happened. Mattie, who had talked of knowing a Dago Joe (but no Dago Mike) during her gangster days in Kansas City, told authorities she knew nothing of Banta or his death.

Nixon eventually was convicted, but the Kansas governor pardoned him three years into a life sentence. He then landed in a state mental hospital, where he died in 1927.

* * *

To say Mattie became bitter in prison is an understatement.

"They put me in a dungeon, but it didn't change me," she said. "They starved me and punished me, but it didn't do any good. I hated them. I came to hate Christians. I hated the world.

"The Christians would come to see me and stand and stare at me. They would get down on their knees and pray, and then go away without once offering to help me."

The Pathway of Mattie Howard devotes a large section to the unfair and cruel treatment of her and the other inmates, including the time she spent in what the book referred to as the "blind cell," a dungeon-like place of total darkness.

Another of the book's favorite topics is Mattie's difficulties with "the colored girls," as she repeatedly referred to them.

She had several run-ins with Black inmates, who the book said "just about ran the place." Mattie complained to the warden about issues ranging from smuggled cigarettes to Blacks charging whites for pressing their dresses, and she went over the warden's head about one issue: the intimacies between the races.

"Not only were there kissing and embracing between the colored and white girls, but they indulged in familiarities unfit to print," the book said. She sent a letter to the State Welfare League, which led to prison officials declaring that Blacks and whites no longer would take recreation periods at the same time.

Needless to say, none of this made her popular among her fellow prisoners. But she still had some friends on the outside.

In her early days behind bars, Mattie remained on the mailing lists of her outlaw cohorts, who sent her flowers, jewelry, candy, and more. Her sister and mother also sent her treats, and Mrs. Howard wrote regularly. She even made the trip from New Mexico to visit occasionally.

Mrs. Howard's letters dwelled on religion and faith and such, which found an unreceptive audience in Mattie. She had several opportunities to find the Lord in prison, and she spurned each one.

Mattie, who still considered herself Catholic, attended the prison's Protestant services, but instead of worshiping she threw wads of paper and balls of bread at the speakers. When a Black prisoner continually sang spirituals in the women's cell block, Mattie yelled at her to shut up.

She even rebuffed a sweet, white-haired woman known as Mother Clark, who visited the imprisoned women and prayed for them. During one meeting, an inmate queried the group: "Well, I wonder where we will all be ten years from now."

"Mrs. Clark looked up at me and said, 'Well, Mattie, you will be preaching the Gospel in ten years,'" Mattie said years later.

"At this I shouted with derision. Of all the hardened sinners by reputation, why should I be singled out for such a ridiculous future. I thought, 'If there was a God, He certainly didn't spend any time around penal institutions, not to my knowledge.'"

Mother Clark couldn't pierce Mattie's tough exterior, much less persuade her to turn to the ways of the Lord. Her response when Mother Clark discussed religion around her was straightforward: "Oh, dry up."

* * *

Nearly five years into her sentence, circumstances improved for Mattie. She and all the other female prisoners were moved from within the walls of the penitentiary and its deplorable conditions to the nearby Missouri Prison Farm, with dormitories, a remodeled farmhouse, and farm animals. Mattie was in charge of the chickens.

Running the farm were an elderly husband and wife whom the prisoners referred to as

Mattie Howard thrived briefly on the Missouri Prison Farm, where she was photographed with the granddaughter of a prison attendant. *Linn County Budget-Gazette, June 28, 1933*

"Daddy" and "Mother," and who were much easier to get along with

than Mattie's nemesis, Matron Smith. Mattie took to her new sur-
roundings, and her behavior improved.

After checking in on Mattie during this period, I was convinced she
was a changed woman. And I wasn't the only one. A prison official said
Mattie had transformed from being "fractious, disobedient, rebellious"
to being a model prisoner.

"She lost sixty days of good time in one big splurge one day for
insolence and profanity," the official said. "She cut loose on an orgy of
swearing, and what a talent Mattie had in that latter line. But now,
everything is different. Mattie doesn't seem like the same girl. All of
our women are out at the farm now. Mattie likes our matron and
is an enormous influence for good and the maintenance of discipline
under her.

"You see, Mattie is a natural leader. She is of the type that always
commands those about her, and she always will be."

Well, maybe not.

"Daddy" and "Mother" departed, with a superintendent taking
over who was decidedly less agreeable. *The Pathway of Mattie Howard*
described him as "a man of low character, sensuous, and possessing a
large, protruding abdomen" and said he was determined "to have his
way with her." After one advance, Mattie smacked him on the head
with a bucket and jabbed him with a pitchfork.

The old Mattie was back. She proceeded to kill all the chickens and
set fire to the chicken coop. She stuck thumb tacks into the cows. She
got into fights with fellow inmates.

Then Mattie had an unexpected visitor.

"I never saw my father sober once in his life until the day he came
to prison before he died and said, 'Forgive me,' and I said, 'No, I will
never forgive you.'

"He said, 'I see the folly of my life. I wish to make amends for
my life.'"

He then told her that he had been saved by Jesus in San Francisco.

"So, he got a burden in his heart to ask me, in prison, to forgive him,
and he came and pleaded with me to forgive him. I had been in the

penitentiary six years and was rather hard, and the matron came and reasoned with me and said, 'Listen, Dear, the day might come when you might want forgiveness.'

"'Well,' I said, 'if it will make him feel better, I will forgive him.'"

Mattie put her arm around her father and kissed him as he left the prison farm. She never saw him again. Charles P. Howard died while Mattie was still incarcerated.

* * *

I was waiting when Mattie walked out of prison on the morning of May 17, 1928, six-and-half years into her twelve-year sentence. I wrote that she was heavier and "lacking some of her old-time luster and physical charm."

"And her hair, which used to coil like a golden crown upon her head, is now merely blond — short and decidedly faded from the tresses that once contributed to her underworld renown as 'the Golden Girl.'"

She wasn't aware her parole had been approved until reading about it in that morning's edition of *The Times*.

She might have figured her parole request had zero chance, but the state prison board thought differently. It released the mattress-burning, scissor-throwing, Christian-hating, chicken-killing inmate five-and-a-half years early under a merit parole for good behavior. Was it possible prison officials just wanted to wash their hands of her?

"I wasn't released because I deserved it," Mattie said, "for I was plenty ornery down there."

As matron Bertha S. Stivers accompanied her to the main prison building, a smiling Mattie wore a light blue dress, blue coat, and black satin pumps, all purchased when the two women had gone shopping.

A prison official asked Mattie, who was now 33, if she would go straight.

"Oh, yes," she replied. "Everybody should go straight, don't you think?"

| 15 |

Chicago

"I was released from the Missouri penitentiary, still bitter and ready to make up for lost time. Chicago, Detroit, New York, and the Eastern gangsters soon grew to know the name of Mattie Howard. The years of 1929 and 1930 found me deeply steeped in the iniquities of these outcasts from justice."
Mattie Howard, *Linn County Budget-Gazette*, June 28, 1933

Mattie Howard immediately went to see her mother, who had moved from Raton to Denver. And, true to her word, she went straight.

For about two weeks.

Mattie and Martha Howard hadn't seen each other in two years, and when Mattie arrived on Martha's Denver doorstep both women wept as they hugged. Upon seeing how frail her mother was, Mattie decided she would make up for the years of suffering she had caused the most important person in her life and vowed never to leave her again.

But...

When she couldn't find work and neighbors, acquaintances, and even some family members treated her with suspicion and hostility, Mattie's will began to weaken. Then she ran into an old friend of her former lover, Albert Pagel. The man took Mattie, who was broke, to dinner one evening. When they got together again, he urged her to meet up with him in Chicago, giving her the cash she would need to make the trip.

The next day, Mattie said goodbye from the back of a taxi as her mother waved farewell from the doorway of her house.

In Chicago, she returned to the lavish lifestyle she had enjoyed ten years earlier in Kansas City, living alone in a well-appointed apartment on fashionable Lake Shore Drive. She also took an active role in bank robberies, bootlegging, and other illegal activities.

I drove cars for the bandits in big cities, helped them rob banks and dispose of their money, helped them to rob jewelry stores, took the jewels to the wholesale houses and sold them, and they would turn around and sell them (back) to the jewelers. If I told all I knew, there would be judges and bankers involved.

There was still interest in Mattie in Kansas City, so it was worth reporting when I learned she was in Chicago. I wrote on December 8, 1928, that the newly minted ex-con not only was living in the Windy City, but also was married, "comparatively happy," and living a normal life.

Well, at least I had the Chicago part right.

It seems likely that, unlike her days as "Queen of the Underworld" in Kansas City, Mattie was at best a duchess in Chicago's gangster hierarchy. But that's still saying something. These were the days when Chicago was the world capital of criminal craziness.

She lived in the city when the St. Valentine's Day Massacre took place on February 14, 1929. In fact, her name was tied briefly to that fateful day on which seven associates of George "Bugs" Moran's North Side Gang were gunned down — by Al Capone's South Side Gang, according to most accounts.

Police suspected Fred "Killer" Burke in the killings, and in December 1929 they tracked him to St. Joseph, Michigan, where he killed a policeman and fled the scene. Law enforcement officers conducted a nationwide manhunt for Burke. Meanwhile, St. Joseph police arrested a woman who had posed as his wife for more than a year.

The local cops insisted the woman was Mattie Howard, and they identified her as such in newspaper stories across the country. Mattie's latest stay in the limelight lasted less than twenty-four hours before the local prosecutor announced the suspect was another woman.

I've had diamonds — big ones. Two- and three-carat diamonds. I've had big, speedy automobiles — Duesenburgs, Cadillacs, and Packards; I've worn sixteen-hundred-dollar capes of ermine; I've lived in apartments on Lake Shore Drive in Chicago. But with all of these I was always seeking something, always searching and seeking some new pleasure. I never found it.

It was a time filled with brief stints in jail and ever-changing aliases as her friends bribed police, judges, and politicians to grease the inner workings of their operations. This was Prohibition in the Windy City, which made even wide-open Kansas City appear tame by comparison.

Based on most accounts, Mattie played a considerably less prominent role in the Chicago underworld than she had in Kansas City. She appears to have been a classic "gangster moll," a term popularized (along with "gun moll") during the 1920s and 1930s that referred to a female running mate — frequently a wife or girlfriend — of a male gangster.

In that capacity, Mattie was used as bait for a robbery victim, flirting with him so that her cohorts could rob and beat him.

She posed as a blind woman to see how much money she could collect begging. She drove getaway cars, sometimes racing away from a fusillade of gunfire by police and sometimes returning fire with a machine gun. On one job, a bullet struck the forefinger of her left hand. On another, she lost control of the car she was driving and it rolled over.

Mattie was the getaway driver after a bank holdup when, with police in hot pursuit firing away, she felt warm fluid splash her hands as she gripped the steering wheel. She saw a cohort slump beside her in his seat, and blood from his wounds began gushing all over her. After eluding the police, she stopped the car at the command of the other holdup men, who pulled their associate's body from the front seat and tossed it on the side of the road.

The lifestyle wore away at Mattie, who began drinking to excess and entertaining thoughts of death before finally telling her gangster friends she needed a break.

I told the gang I was going to find a job and quit them. They howled with glee. "You, Mattie Howard, the notorious agate-eyed moll of the underworld, companion of the largest cities' most undesirable citizens, where could you find work?" But I tried honestly. I had three nice jobs in succession, until the insurance people found I was working for these people.

Her depression worsened to the point where she made a half-hearted attempt at suicide, slashing her forearm with a razor blade. She survived with a few stitches.

By mid-1931, Mattie realized it was time to follow a different path, a path that would take her away from Chicago. But it still didn't lead her to God or religion.

I thought all Christians were hypocrites and that there wasn't any God. I became bitter, and the bitterness became corroded. I decided to go back home to Denver and Mother and do as she had always hoped I would.

When Mattie arrived in Denver, she learned her mother had died nine days earlier.

| 16 |

Return to Kansas City

"I remember an elderly woman who prayed for me in the old days. And everything she asked of God was granted. I thought she was goofy. Thank God, I'm goofy like that."
Mattie Howard, *The Kansas City Star,* March 1, 1933

Mattie Howard contacted me in October 1932 to say she had experienced a genuine conversion.

While pushing a broom.

Using the name Tossel Lee, she had found a job as a governess for a well-to-do family in a fashionable section of Denver. She cared for two children, ages two and three.

"I grew to love these babies and their mother," she said. "... But all the time I was under a terrific strain. What if someone who knew me should see me and learn of my assumed name? What if something should happen in the house while I was employed there?"

She continually battled the urge to drink liquor, sometimes giving in, and struggled with feelings of depression. But then, like a bolt from on high, it happened.

Mattie's employers were out of town, leaving her in charge of the two children. They were playing in the rear of the house one morning while she was in the front cleaning.

I tuned in on the radio while sweeping the floor. I heard a string quartet playing church music, "Sweet Hour of Prayer," and then the voice of the minister, S.H. Patterson, preaching. ... When the voice of the speaker said, "Let us pray," I suddenly found myself on my knees beside the divan, calling from my heart to this Jehovah, who could and would do things for a sinner like me. My broom lay unheeded beside me, as the tears swept down my face, and for the first time in my life I really sent up a plea to the Almighty. ... I could see clearly once more.

The Rev. Patterson invited listeners to visit Radio Prayer League Church, and Mattie did so, leaving the children with a neighbor lady. She returned to the church two nights later, but Patterson wasn't leading the services. Mattie recognized the preacher as Joe Kenny, a notorious prisoner at the Missouri State Penitentiary who had led multiple attempted prison breaks. He was now known as the Rev. Dan McNally.

After listening to him preach about how God had led the children of Israel out of Egypt, Mattie left her perch in the church balcony and approached him. She knelt, and McNally lowered himself beside her.

"God bless you, Sister. Pray through, be sure," he said.

"Don't you know me? I'm Mattie Howard," she said.

"Well, may God bless you!" the preacher replied.

The two ex-cons chatted a bit longer.

"Why don't you try God. He helped me," McNally said.

"You're right. I'm going to let the whole world know who I am. By the grace of God, I am going to go on."

Try God, indeed.

I stood up before that assembly of 750 people, and, unashamed, I told them I had deceived them, that I was not Miss Tossel Lee, but the ex-convict, Mattie Howard, whose misdeeds had been blazoned from every newspaper in the country and whose crime was that of murder. I wasn't guilty of that crime, but my term in prison had repaid for many other sins I had committed.

As with her immersion into the criminal underworld, Mattie plowed full steam ahead with her foray into the spiritual world.

First, she gave testimony at a Sunday school, then at a church service. Then at another church service. As word of this ex-convict's conversion spread, she again became a wanted woman — now by pastors at churches all over Colorado who wanted Mattie to speak to their congregations.

Patterson and McNally even arranged for her to address a crowd of about three thousand at the Denver Auditorium.

Meanwhile, her employers had returned. Tossel Lee confessed to the mother of the children in her charge that her real name was Mattie Howard and that she had spent time in the Missouri penitentiary.

"I suppose I had better get out now?" Mattie said.

"No, indeed," the woman replied. "You have proven yourself in my home, and I don't care if you have served twenty years. You can stay here as long as you want to.

"I love you from the tip of your toes to the top of your head. The Lord has softened your heart."

Mattie's employer showed her confidence by opening an account in Mattie's name at an up-scale Denver store. Mattie charged a pair of shoes.

Having made the trip to Denver to chronicle her conversion, I sat across from Mattie in the offices of the Radio Prayer League Church. She wanted folks in Kansas City to hear her story.

"I'd like to go back to Kansas City and thank the people who were kind to me," she told me.

My story described her as wearing "a plain, near blue, serge dress. ... Her features have changed. She wore no makeup or rouge. Her hands are calloused from hard, but honest toil. But she is supremely happy in her new life and looked it. Her eyes flashed, and a contagious smile frequently swept over her face as she told her story."

McNally was pastor at the Heart of America Gospel Center in Kansas City, so he was able to make Mattie's wish to return to the scene of her many crimes come true. She arrived on February 23, 1933, in advance of her revival at the church at 29th Street and Prospect Avenue.

* * *

Mattie was making headlines again in Kansas City — but her companion now was God rather than gangsters.

"'The Girl with Agate Eyes' Says Hymn Led Her to God"

"Mattie Howard on Gospel"

"Her 'Agate Eyes' Softer"

"Mattie Not Going Back"

"A Pardon from Christ"

This Mattie was a far cry from the ingenue who arrived in Kansas City in 1917. She was thirty-eight years old and on the stout side. She wore no makeup, though her blond hair remained fashionably coiffed.

She preached to thousands of worshipers over nearly a month at the Heart of America Gospel Center, a few blocks east of where her lover Albert Pagel had suffered a mortal gunshot wound during an attempted bank robbery thirteen years earlier.

Friends in Denver had warned her against coming to Kansas City.

"They told me I was foolish to try to go to Kansas City," Mattie said to her audience. "It was here that I was arrested every time the police saw me. Why, one day I was in jail and out fifteen times.

"My friends said I had no money and that my 'flivver' took gasoline. I told them I didn't care, that I was going to Kansas City, and here I am."

Mattie began her revival at the Heart of America Gospel Center on February 26 and drew an overflow crowd, as she did for almost all her Kansas City appearances. Newspaper reporters covered several of them.

I witnessed one of her first sermons. The auditorium was filled to hear Mattie speak, and an overflow of would-be worshipers listened on a loudspeaker in the basement.

Mattie was now an evangelist, and she had the look of an evangelist, pacing back and forth, jabbing a finger here or shaking a fist there for emphasis as she addressed the congregation.

The men who knew The Girl with the Agate Eyes in her heyday weren't buying it.

"Come on back and cut the comedy, Mattie," Kansas City gangsters wrote to her.

Other friends "sat around with their chins in their hands, staring at me," she said. "'This can't be Mattie,' they'd say, 'she's gone crazy or something.'"

But she insisted this was no act.

"I'm pardoned," she bellowed with tears running down her cheeks. "All my past is pardoned, not by the state but by Jesus Christ."

On hand one night was Harry Arthur, the police detective who had arrested Mattie and had escorted her and Sam Taylor by train from Trinidad, Colorado, to Kansas City in 1918. Arthur said Mattie had once sent a gunman to Kansas City to "put him on the spot," but he learned of the plot and avoided a bloody death. He didn't seem to hold that against her now.

Mattie's sermons were fashioned around her compelling story and simple themes. She urged her congregation to give up cigarettes, liquor, gambling, and dancing.

"I know what they lead to. ... I know something about drinking. I've taken on more whiskey than any man in town. Leave the cards alone. Forget about dancing. Get the grace of the Lord, and when you get the grace of the Lord, you've got something."

Near the end of Mattie's evangelistic gatherings at the Heart of America Gospel Center, McNally said she had been responsible for more than 200 conversions.

"I have become a trumpet of the Lord. From sin I have turned to glory. ... That's why my eyes are no longer of agate."

* * *

Mattie peered through the iron bars inside the Jackson County Jail, where she had spent so many days and nights before, during, and after her murder trial in 1919.

It was March 4, 1933, and Mattie was at the jail to comfort Paul Kauffman, who had been sentenced to death for the murder of seventeen-year-old Avis Woolery.

"I want to see him about his soul," Mattie told the chief deputy sheriff.

He led her to the third floor, where she stood before Kauffman in his cell.

"Since I have given myself to God, all hate and malice is gone from my heart," she told him. "Will you kneel as I pray?"

The convicted murderers knelt together.

"Promise me that you will continue praying," she said.

"I promise," he said.

Sheriff Tom Bash invited Mattie to extend her visit, so she shared her story of crime and conversion with other inmates. Mattie, who insisted she be allowed inside the cells, knelt on newspapers as she prayed with them.

"Grant that these may see the error of their ways and be led to peace that is of Thee, even as I was."

She promised them everlasting joy if they would believe.

After leaving the jail, Mattie walked to the nearby courthouse where she had been convicted of murder. She chatted with a former janitor and a deputy marshal, thanking them for their kindness during her stay in the jail. She gave each a photograph of herself in her evangelist's garb.

The photo carried the caption, "From prison to pulpit."

| 17 |

Epilogue

*"I've had money and everything that money would buy —
motor cars, jewels, apartments, furs, clothes — but I wouldn't
trade all of them for the peace and joy that is mine now."*
Mattie Howard, *The Kansas City Times*, February 27, 1933

A t the time Mattie Howard broke into evangelism, Aimee Semple
McPherson represented the gold standard.

Known to her followers as "Sister," McPherson was born in Canada
in 1890 (four years before the birth of Mattie) and began preaching
in 1915. In 1918 (the year Mattie was charged with the murder of Joe
Morino), she moved to Los Angeles, where she established the International Church of the Foursquare Gospel, earning a following of tens
of thousands — as well as considerable wealth and notoriety.

She built her 5,300-seat Angelus Temple in Los Angeles in 1923.
Considered the world's first megachurch, the Angelus Temple is where
Mattie reached the pinnacle of her preaching career.

In May 1937, McPherson chose Mattie to conduct a monthlong revival. The *Foursquare Crusader*, billed as the "Official Organ of the International Church of the Foursquare," said in its May 5, 1937, edition:

"Rev. Mattie Howard is known from coast to coast as the converted
convict and gangsters' associate. But her message is more than just a

novelty. She is one good preacher, with a wide and varied experience with life, both as a dyed-in-the-wool sinner and as an able and color-ful evangelist. She comes to Angels Temple for a month of services — services that are different, mellow, and above all, profitable."

The *Crusader* said Mattie "believes that some six thousand souls have found Christ through her ministry." Ensuing editions printed excerpts from her sermons. They were sprinkled with the fire and brimstone you would expect from an evangelist, but Mattie mostly regaled the crowds with stories of her days as a gangster.

Drinking, smoking, gambling, philandering, dancing — she and her outlaw friends enjoyed them all at one time, and she decried them all now. She condemned the acts, but not the actors. Of her former associates, she said, "They are some of the nicest people in the world, but they need salvation."

Many found death instead. Mattie's running mates Dale Jones, Frank Lewis, Blackie Lancaster, Tony Cruye, Spider Kelly, and George Evans all died between 1918 and 1920, as did her lover, Albert Pagel. But the curse of Mattie Howard didn't end there. Two other men who played important roles in her life, Sam Taylor and the Rev. Dan McNally, also died prematurely and tragically.

Taylor, who like Mattie was convicted in the killing of Joe Morino, survived the bloody days of 1918-1920 but faced a life sentence in the Missouri State Penitentiary. He was paroled in 1933, thanks in part to a letter of support from newly minted evangelist Mattie Howard.

Writing from Colorado, Mattie told the prison board that Taylor "was absolutely innocent of the crime" and that she had "good reason to believe the perpetrator of the crime is now dead." She likely was refer-ring to Dale Jones, who considerable evidence suggested was the culprit and who had died in a shootout with police in November 1918.

As had become her custom, Mattie also took the opportunity to emphasize her own innocence.

Also writing on Taylor's behalf was James P. Aylward, a well-respected Kansas City lawyer who had helped convict Mattie during her murder trial. The estate of Joe Morino had hired Aylward as a special assistant to the prosecution, which insisted during the trial that Mattie and Taylor had teamed up to murder Morino.

Now Aylward was changing his tune. He wrote to the prison board that he doubted Taylor had played any part in the murder, which was exactly what the Kansas City police chief had said shortly after Taylor's 1918 arrest in Colorado.

So, perhaps justice finally prevailed — albeit after Taylor spent thirteen years in the state pen.

Upon leaving prison, he jumped on the evangelistic bandwagon and became a preacher. One of his first acts was to seek absolution from at least some of those he had wronged during his gangster days.

In July 1934, he entered a Kansas City grocery store and approached the proprietor, Max Cohen, who stood behind the counter.

"This is a peculiar mission I have, Mr. Cohen," Taylor said. "I want to ask your forgiveness for blowing your safe sixteen years ago."

"Do you have the money — the $340 in cash alone — that I lost?" Cohen asked.

Taylor didn't.

"Well, I can't forgive you."

Taylor not only left without absolution, he also wound up in jail. Two cops arrested Taylor in his home later in the day and hauled him off on a charge of burglary brought by Cohen.

"Of all the nerve," Taylor said. "When I was trying to do the right thing, too."

The county prosecutor's office quickly ordered him to be released because the statute of limitations on the crime had expired.

Taylor died less than three years later when a train rammed into the car he was driving at a railroad crossing in Glade Springs, Virginia. He was on his way to a series of evangelical meetings in Pennsylvania.

McNally, who had inspired Mattie's conversion and evolution into evangelist, met his own tragic death.

The man known as Joe Kenny when he was a prisoner at the Missouri penitentiary bought a plane and began billing himself as "The Flying Evangelist" in 1940. Within months, he was killed along with his wife and daughter when his plane crashed shortly after takeoff in Binghamton, New York.

* * *

You might guess that Jesse E. James, better known as Jesse James Jr., became a member of the Mattie Howard Bloody Death Club, but he didn't. James lived to be seventy-five years old.

It's safe to say, however, that his life didn't go well after he lost Mattie's murder trial, the biggest case of his legal career. First, his movie career flopped when he gave up the law for Hollywood. Then, he returned to Kansas City a broken and broke man (he had mortgaged his house to help finance the two movies about his father).

In the ensuing years, James moved his family into an apartment, suffered a nervous breakdown, joined the Ku Klux Klan, and was implicated (but never charged) in one of Kansas City's most notorious murders of the 1920s.

Zeo Zoe Wilkins, who had been James's final legal client, was found stabbed to death on the morning of March 16, 1924. Wilkins was widely known in the Midwest for her habit of marrying wealthy men and winding up in possession of their riches through divorce or other means. Her murder was never solved.

The son of Jesse James eventually returned to the West Coast, where he battled mental illness during the latter half of his life. He died March 26, 1951, in Los Angeles and was buried in the famous Forest Lawn Memorial Park in Glendale, California.

* * *

From Shamokin, Pennsylvania, to Deadwood, South Dakota, and from Elmira, New York, to Fresno, California, Mattie was promoted as "God's Miracle Woman," "Queen of the Bandits," and "The Girl from Gangland" as evangelism took her from coast to coast and beyond — she preached in Honolulu in 1946.

Newspaper reports indicated that during her evangelistic days, she lived in Denver, Detroit, Minneapolis, and Portland, Oregon. In

Minneapolis, she founded a church called the Little Chapel, complete with a radio broadcast, and established an employment agency for young women.

During a sermon a few years after her conversion, the woman who had been very publicly linked to multiple lovers in her bad-girl days said she had sworn off the opposite sex. She said men had no place in her life except in God's work.

"Regardless of the reports being circulated about me, I'm not married and don't ever intend to be," she said. "I'm giving all my time to God."

As far as can be determined from newspaper stories and official records, Mattie stuck to that pledge and never remarried after her divorce from Frank J. Vanders was finalized in 1920. She also never had children.

Final notes

Mattie Howard died on November 9, 1984, two days before her ninetieth birthday, after spending her final years in the Los Angeles area.

William Moorhead, the longtime police reporter for *The Kansas City Star*, had died three years earlier, also at the age of eighty-nine.

Thanks to:

My wife Sue Kelly, sister and brother-in-law Mary Kay and Frank Richter, and brother and sister-in-law Steve and Debbi Kelly for their input and opinions. Rebecca Wagner of the Kansas City Art Institute for her cover illustration. And Maria Martin for her meticulous proofreading.

Also:

    National Archives of Kansas City
    Missouri State Archives
    Missouri State Historical Society
    Midwest Genealogy Center
    Kansas City Public Library
    Mid-Continent Public Library
    Kenneth Spencer Research Library Archival Collections at the University of Kansas

Newspaper sources:

    The Kansas City Star
    The Kansas City Times
    The Kansas City Post
    The Kansas City Journal
    The Kansas City Kansan

Foursquare Crusader
Los Angeles Times
Los Angeles Herald
Linn County (Missouri) Budget-Gazette
Holt County (Missouri) Sentinel
The Butler (Missouri) Weekly Times
The Springfield (Missouri) Leader and Press
Springfield (Missouri) Daily Leader
The Daily Capital News (Jefferson City, Missouri)
Jefferson City (Missouri) Post-Tribune
St. Joseph (Missouri) Gazette
The Leavenworth (Kansas) Post
The Leavenworth (Kansas) Times
The Coffeyville (Kansas) Daily Journal
The Hutchinson (Kansas) News
Des Moines (Iowa) Tribune
The Des Moines (Iowa) Register
The Pueblo (Colorado) Chieftan
The Salt Lake (Utah) Tribune
The Standard-Sentinel (Stillwell, Oklahoma)
The Ogden (Utah) Standard-Examiner
Star-Tribune (Minneapolis, Minnesota)
Press and Sun-Bulletin (Binghamton, New York)
The News-Herald (Franklin, Pennsylvania)
The Baltimore Sun
The Cincinnati Post
Atlanta Constitution
The Buffalo (New York) Times
Akron (Ohio) Beacon Journal
The Indianapolis Star
San Francisco Chronicle

Bibliography

The Pathway of Mattie Howard (To and from Prison): True Story of the Regeneration of an Ex-Convict and Gangster Woman by M. Harris, copyright by Mattie Howard, 1937

Kill-Crazy Gang: The Crimes of the Lewis-Jones Gang by Jeffrey S. King, 2013

The Love Pirate and the Bandit's Son by Laura James, 2009

Son of a Bandit: Jesse James & the Leeds Gang by Ralph Monaco II, 2012

Police Reporter by William Moorhead, 1955

Aimee Semple McPherson and the Resurrection of Christian America by Matthew Avery Sutton, 2007

De Valera in America: The Rebel President and the Making of Irish Independence by Dave Hannigan, 2008

Human Wolves: Seventeen Years of War on Crime by Lear B. Reed, 1941

Deaths on Pleasant Street by Giles Fowler, 2009

Wide-Open Town: Kansas City in the Pendergast Era by Diane Mutti Burke, Jason Roe, and John Herron, editors, 2018

Black Hand/Strawman: The History of Organized Crime in Kansas City by Terence Michael O'Malley, 2011

Lawman to Outlaw: Verne Miller and the Kansas City Massacre by Brad Smith, 2003

Kansas City: An American Story by Rick Montgomery and Shirl Kasper, 1999

Kansas City Chronicles: An Up-to-Date History by David Jackson, 2010

Kansas City Crime Central: 150 Years of Outlaws, Kidnappers, Mobsters and Their Victims by Monroe Dodd, 2010

The Mafia and the Machine: The Story of the Kansas City Mob by Frank R. Hayde, 2007

Storied & Scandalous Kansas City: A History of Corruption, Mischief and a Whole Lot of Booze by Karla Deel, 2019

The Girl on the Velvet Swing: Sex, Murder, and Madness at the Dawn of the Twentieth Century by Simon Baatz, 2018

Tiger Girl and the Candy Kid: America's Original Gangster Couple by Glenn Stout, 2021

The Girls of Murder City: Fame, Lust, and the Beautiful Killers who inspired "Chicago" by Douglas Perry, 2010

The Girl with the Agate Eyes: The Life and Times of Mattie Howard, Master of Arts thesis at University of Oklahoma by Michael Ballif, 2022

American Midnight: The Great War, a Violent Peace, and Democracy's Forgotten Crisis by Adam Hochschild, 2022

CPSIA information can be obtained
at www.ICGtesting.com
Printed in the USA
LVHW011148220723
753114LV00014B/1552